PERFECT MIND PERFECT SOUL

M. R. WESTERTERP

PERFECT MIND PERFECT SOUL
www.perfectmindperfectsoul.com

The contents of this book are solely intended as reference materials only and
not as medical or professional advice. Portions of the information contained
herein are intended to give you the tools to make informed decisions about
your wellbeing. The information contained herein should not be used as a
substitute for any treatment that has been prescribed or recommended by your
doctor or medical practitioner.

72-14CE1811

Edited by Brenda Garriss (brendagarriss.com)

Published by TOTA Publishing Inc.

ISBN: 978-0-9917151-0-7

Special thanks to Brenda Garriss, for her tireless effort and assistance bringing this body of work forward.

TABLE OF CONTENTS

Chapter 1 • THE ARCHITECT

What if you could wipe the architecture of your life clean, leaving you with a fresh blueprint to redesign it?

Would you take the opportunity?

Would you be willing to take the steps to get there?

We are all architects of our own personal fate and responsible for our misdirections in life.

It is the lack of understanding and inability to discover one's "soul purpose" that will scatter the lines of one's blueprint, creating confusion and making it virtually impossible to recognize the correct paths laid out before them.

When we are able to separate ourselves from our own self made conditions we are able to see more clearly, allowing us to build a stronger foundation for our journey.

We all need to understand the reason for our existence. Without purpose, we are wandering aimlessly, as a ship without an anchor. The first step in redefining our personal blueprint is learning how to control the processes that create the confusion and misdirections in our lives. Upon doing so, one will begin to discover a whole new world opening up, bringing forward a more positive outlook and future; a world of greater understanding and knowledge.

As you proceed through these pages, it is the hope that you will discover a higher vibration that will guide you and place you on a path of empowerment which allows you to create wise choices in life, and subsequently, shows you how to find your peace, the Light within.

Most importantly, you will be provided with the tools to assist you in shining your light brightly and allowing yourself to be a beacon to others so that they too will have the desire to seek the Light for themselves. Additionally, you will learn how to protect your light so that no man, woman or child will ever have the power to extinguish it.

This is about self empowerment and achieving your purpose on this earth plane.

So many people are travelling through life totally oblivious as to why they are here. They continuously seek the meaning of their existence, and wonder what's next. We observe them mindlessly participating in their daily lives with blank expressions on their faces, their eyes, allowing you to see inside their soul and it's empty.

We were created with a spark inside us that is designed to connect us to our Spiritual bodies. It is the source of our divinity. We need only to ignite this spark once again and allow it to burn brightly to see. Through this action, we will empower ourselves to rid that which enslaves us, medicates us, controls or abuses us, that which is the source of our fear.

Chapter 2 • ENERGY

Our divinity is real; it is housed in our body, our vessel. It is located in the area known as the solar plexus, which is located just above the abdomen and just below where your rib cages meet in the middle. We quite often have sensations in this area when conversing with others or when we are found in an emotional situation. These sensations may vary from excitement to being physically nauseous. This is where the expression "go with your gut" comes from. One should pay attention carefully to these signs, because it is our divinity speaking to us.

Have you ever noticed that when you are conversing with someone who is speaking negatively, that you quite often cross your arms over your solar plexus? This is your spirit subconsciously telling you to protect your divinity. If we don't protect it, we will absorb the negative energy being expelled by other individuals.

If you can grasp the concept of energy and how it works then you are well on your way to discovering your divine power. How you wish to use this energy is up to you, we all have free will. But know one thing; whatever gets sent out always comes back!

Energy is invisible. Most people are oblivious to its existence and many that are aware of it need to understand the Universal or Natural Laws that govern how this energy should and will be used. As you go forward you will notice references to Universal or Natural Law. These are one in the same and used interchangeably.

Universal Laws have been in place since the beginning of creation. These pages bring no one's religion to the table, but rather present these truths as being the Creation, Creator or God of your understanding. Universal Laws are immutable, which means that no man or spirit entity can change these laws, nor can they be modified to serve one's personal agenda. There is not a single court on the earth plane that has any control or power over these laws; these laws have power over them. This is no big secret; but rather common sense, with a better understanding.

Nature follows Natural Law. Plants, trees, animals all have a cycle of life and a purpose, as do humans. They follow a circular pattern, which gives their strength. The circle is the strongest shape in nature. The planets are circular, they spin in a circular motion, and they orbit in a circular fashion around each other. Our seasons of spring, summer, winter and fall are circular. The cycle of life is circular; we originate in spirit form, arriving as an infant, proceeding to our youth, adulthood, eldership and finally return back to spirit form.

Nature also has a harmonious blend in its circles; the soil, sun, and rain feeds the plants, seeds fall and new plants grow to repeat the same cycle. As we can observe, nature is constantly showing us the strength of the circle and teaching us how to become in harmony with our own natural creation.

Nature completes its cycles from year to year and thrives in abundance. Man seems to be the only species that affects this cycle negatively, interfering with greed and ignorance and destroying that which is designed to teach us and give us life.

Nature will always correct itself, as it always remains in balance with the universe. Man needs to observe this perfection for through this we will have a greater understanding of the impact and destruction that we cause. We must learn how to become in compliance with the Laws of Nature so that we too can thrive in abundance provided by these same laws.

Nature never lies to us. Valuable lessons from the circle of life are taught by nature. We need to be awakened from our sleep and pay attention to the signs we are being shown. Man is not the height of intelligence on this earth plane, nature is. This explains why many individuals choose to ignore the lessons nature offers us. We should not be ignorant; we should be more open to learning and understanding.

There are many truths hidden in nature that man is not permitted to discover, as man's lust for greed and power would only destroy that which keeps nature in balance. It is a deliberate act that the spiritual realm keeps much hidden from man. They only permit those who have earned the trust of the spirit forces access to these tools. These trusted individuals will never stand on stages revealing these mysteries, as they are shown for a purpose, serve their purpose and humbly disappear into the silence. They seek no glory or profit; this is why they have been chosen.

So with this simple understanding it is easy to see that if one becomes in harmony with Natural Law, that individual will open up a new pathway of knowledge and personal empowerment. This is the path that leads us toward burning our divinity brightly and harnessing that to which we are all entitled in this material world.

Now with this basic understanding, there are some simple rules to energy. Energy is very real. Because we don't actually see energy we tend to disregard it. It is important to understand that energy is as real as a blade of grass or a young puppy. If we feed that blade of grass or that puppy it will grow, as does energy.

Thought is energy and how we control our thoughts interprets the kind of energy that we send out into the world and into the universe.

Energy moves in a circular fashion around us. For example, you could be sitting there thinking about someone you know that mistreated you in some way. Perhaps it's something that person may have said or done that irritated you. So you begin to think; "I hate that person, I hope he fails in life, I hope something bad happens to him".

What you have just done is create negative energy in the universe with your thoughts. This energy is now alive and will manifest forward. This energy goes out across the grid and it reaches this person. You have created an energy connection between yourself and this individual. It penetrates their being with the negative energy you sent and now has the power to cause many adverse things to happen to this individual. They will now be consumed with this negative energy that you have sent them and may begin to exhibit behaviors of nervousness, anger, anxiety, negativity, or depression.

At that very moment, this individual may begin to think of you in a negative fashion as well. You have created an energy connection within the universe. You can be thousands of miles apart; space is irrelevant, universal energy travels with great speed and is felt instantly. You have now started a magnification and this energy begins to grow between the two of you.

Now, Natural Law states that this energy is not allowed to just hang out in the Universe. Once it's delivered, it has to go somewhere. Where is that somewhere? It's back to its original owner. Natural Law attaches a nice little gift with it also, it returns it in tenfold. You will now be consumed with the same energy you sent out, only ten times worse. You have now unknowingly created your own negative condition around yourself. It is difficult for many to stop this negative thought process, they continue repeating hypothetical situations in their mind over and over again of what they "should" have done or said. These are all just hypothetical thought processes that will never occur, and so they end up being wasted energy. You may experience a temporary "high" from your actions and initially it may make you feel good, but this self created negativity will rapidly crash in full force in your own energy field, leaving you tired and depressed.

There are some people who prefer to live this way in life. The majority of words they speak and thoughts they send out on a daily basis are negative. They enjoy living in this condition; they are blinded to what they are actually doing to themselves. These individuals are stuck in life and cannot move ahead because they constantly defy universal alignment.

Now let's flip the switch. You are sitting there thinking of this person and the thought processes turn more positive. "You know, I may not have fully agreed with what that person said or how he acted, but I am not going to let him get to me. I am not going to let him have my power. I'm going to take the high road and let this go, I do wish him well."

This is a different energy, but Natural Law works in the same fashion, you've given creation to the energy within the universe. The energy is delivered to the individual and absorbed by him. It will change the way in how they think about you, as you have sent this more positive vibration. It will elevate their mood towards you and they will feel an immediate positive connection with you. Their thought processes will be connected with yours at that moment, in a more positive fashion, as you have created this energy connection.

Now, Universal Law states this energy is not allowed to just hang out in the universe. Once it's delivered it must return to its owner and yes, it is attached with a nice little gift, it is returned in tenfold with positive energy towards you. You will now be consumed with the same energy you sent out, only ten times greater.

Now ask yourself a very simple question. Which one do you prefer? You can apply this any way you want in life but know that whatever you send out comes back to you. If you wish to send negative energy all the time then know that you will pay the price. You will be ever so consumed with this negativity that it will destroy your own being and you will end up being a miserable, lonely empty shell at the end of the day.

Think about it; how many times has the thought of somebody from your past just popped into your mind? The reason why it happened, whether good or bad, is because an energy connection of thought processes was created between you and that individual right at that moment in time. Remember, you are not always the creator of the energy; it may have come from this other individual and was sent to you. They may have been thinking about you at that exact moment.

It's very simple to test the theory, how did you immediately feel at that moment in time? Did your own energy suddenly shift? The type of energy you feel (positive, neutral or negative) is determined by how you left your relationship with this person from your past. Did you suddenly feel anger or negativity towards this person? Did you suddenly feel happy or long to see this individual again? This is the energy that exists between the two of you and is flowing back and forth.

Understanding this flow of energy teaches you how an energy connection between humans actually works. If you hold negative thoughts towards another, you become a slave to that person. Learn how to control this energy and you will learn how to better your relationships with those around you.

The burden of stress and anxiety comes from within the thought processes and energy surrounding each individual. We must learn to control this energy for not only the betterment of our own health, but also for the betterment of our mental state of being. As we send these energies out, they will continue to grow and manifest. One thought will lead to another and new thoughts will be created. We must be careful how we create these thoughts, as it is the initial energy that grows and rebounds back to us. Emotions are attached to thought. We control our thinking through our mind chatter or self talk. We can turn our emotions on or off through these thoughts. When negative thoughts enter, we must learn to stop it and send that energy off.

We need to learn how to control the mind chatter, which is where the confusing thought processes originate. We must learn to listen to our own spirit within, which will guide the thought processes. Greater clarity will come. When we encounter conflict in our lives, that is nature's way of telling us, we are not in harmony with our spiritual self.

Without realizing it, many people bring disease upon themselves because they are so consumed with their own negativity. Illness, whether mental or physical, is often self inflicted. Controlling energy is all part of the master alignment, which is a perfect blend of your body with the balance of nature; this is all part of that plan. Though energy may not be a food or an herb, it's equally important to your natural balance, energy is a very powerful force. The main issue is that energy is invisible to the human eye, therefore, many people are oblivious to its existence or they just straight out reject its control in their everyday lives. Thought energy is another of the body's triggers; just as a scent, a visual or a song may trigger memories from your past giving you an instant connection to that event or person.

When one keeps feeding thought energy it continuously magnifies within the body. A mind of wrongful thinking is destructive to the body and mind. The brain acts as a laboratory creating chemicals for the body and if your mind is consumed with negativity then it will create harmful chemicals that will release destructive forces throughout your body and disease will manifest itself over time.

You would have to imagine how this energy travels throughout your body and also into the Universe. It would be similar to putting a drop of blue dye into a glass of water, it will slowly spread out in minute strands until it grows and grows and eventually it consumes that glass of water and replaces the clarity with its blue. Energy works in the exact same fashion.

It is imperative that one learns to control and be responsible for the energy they create. Techniques will be provided later in the book to assist you.

Chapter 3 • THE SPIRIT WORLD

Before we can proceed, there must be a basic understanding of the Spiritual Realm that exists around us. For some, this may be difficult to comprehend and certainly, we each have free will and must make our own decisions in life. But do know that "the spiritual" is part of our life's lessons. The Creator has granted us intelligence to walk this journey and an intuitive ability to know the divine truth within. Divine wisdom is held within the vibration of the energy of the pages you are holding. If this truth does not speak to you then move on, if it does speak to you, you will feel it within and know there is something here for you.

This book was created by the knowledge obtained working with, and through the assistance of, Spirit entities. It has taken many years to attain the information within. It is in no way written by Spirit, and no claims are made as such. They have no books on the earth plane. Anybody who claims to tell you their book is entirely written by Spirit does not speak the truth. Even The Bible was rewritten by man.

You are spirit in manifested physical form. All bodies consist of two life forms. There is the physical vessel or material body and there is the ethereal or spirit body. A life-force in the spirit realm feeds the required amount of energy each day for our vessels to stay functioning. This is the fuel that keeps our hearts pumping.

When we die, or, cease to exist on the earthly world, we no longer have a need for the physical vessel and our spirit form returns back from where it came. Want a reality check? Spirit calls us "low debaste energies". In our earthly state we exist as lower forms of life compared to the spirit realm. This explains why we must become receptive to the "higher intelligences of life". We need to be able to commune with the highest spiritual source for our guidance and attain to align with the higher forms of energy that serve to protect us, for we are them and shall return one day to our rightful place.

Life continues on, it is eternal in spirit form. Spirit calls it a rebirth; we are reborn into the spirit world. Their words; *"we toss aside our earthly vessels like an old t-shirt, we no longer need them."* The physical body is no longer necessary as it is merely a material possession of the earth plane designed by the Creator to house our ethereal (spirit) bodies for its journey here. It's our temple. When it is no longer needed it returns back to where it came from, the earth.

The transition from the earth world back to the spirit world is described by Spirit as; *"you fall asleep in one bed and wake up in another"*.

Are the spirits of our loved ones that have passed before us hanging around the cemeteries? The answer is "no". They don't want to be confined, they would rather be in the car with you as you travel, protecting you along the way. Spirit does not actually even like tombstones left in their remembrance as it creates a lower energy connection, but they understand its part of the human condition and is merely meant for those that are left behind, it serves no purpose for those who have passed on.

Yes, when it is our time to return to the spirit realm we will be reunited with our family members and friends who passed before us, including our pets.

Those who exist in spirit will visit us often to check up on us, as there is a strong energy connection there. They will quite often bring us messages and guidance for our journey.

Is your mother, father, brother, sister, partner, lover still that on the spirit side? Not really. We have come down to the earth plane for many different incarnations and varied lessons. Our spirits were uniquely made by the Creator a very long time ago and we are all on different paths. We've experienced many different family units, friends and partners along the way, which, when one thinks about it, is quite intriguing.

People often say "I wish I had this knowledge when I was younger". As we continue to evolve, we learn how to translate our gathered wisdom from our current life to multiple lifetimes. Our spirit is defined by the knowledge of multiple lifetimes. We are only permitted to bring what is important to our continued growth on this journey, as the rest of the details would be too much of a burden to our fragile human conditions.

Why can't we bring these memories? Simply put, it would be much too painful for our earthly bodies to have to remember everyone from our past journeys, we're not strong enough as humans to handle that condition, and only in spirit form can we understand.

We are all here to participate in lessons of higher learning, which in essence, makes all of us classmates in this Earth School.

It is quite possible, even likely that there is a repeat performance, a mate or sibling during a previous incarnation that returns as our mate or sibling in another. There always is a specific reason for that coupling to be repeated. It all depends on our individual growth paths and our sacred contracts with each other.

Do not be saddened by this, we do meet again and at that time we will have a greater understanding of the whole picture.

Spirit entities have unique identities just as each individual on the earth plane does. Are we all created in his likeness? Spirit says this means; *"we are all created of equality, with the same advantages according to our actions or deeds"*.

The Creator is not an old man with a beard as Sunday School teachers may have alluded. The Godhead is more of an extremely high energy form. Is his/her existence even real? Spirit says the Creator exists.

In the spiritual realm it is said that the Godhead or God Source is a much evolved form of energy with light so powerful that it would blind a human to look into it.

There is no explanation as to what the Creator looks like, as those in spirit cannot describe it to us. We do not possess the words in our earthly languages to understand what they are trying to say to us. They say the interpretation of this is left to the individual. Just as those in the western hemisphere may see Santa Claus with a red suit and grey beard, there are those in the eastern hemisphere that may see Santa Claus entirely different. Spirit says however we interpret the vision of our understanding of the Godhead is irrelevant, as long as we understand our own individual connection to the source of all creation.

When someone around us dies it is normal to grieve, this is a human condition. We must grieve, it is a chemical release within the system. If we hold our sorrow within, illness will beset us later in life. Death is not final though, we are not saying "goodbye", we are merely saying "we'll see you later", for they have only gone on before us and we will meet again.

Much like a loved one or friend may move to another part of the country and be physically absent for many years, we do have the option to see them again one day and we do get to talk to them on the phone. The same is true for our loved ones that pass before us. It has been proven that we are still able to communicate with them and we will get to see them again. This is not supernatural or fictitious, this is reality. Death is just part of the entire life cycle. The capability to communicate with spirit entities absolutely exists.

Some people are terrified if they see a spirit entity or hear a voice of a loved one that has passed into Spirit. Have no fear; they will never do you any harm. They merely have come to visit you or perhaps offer you assistance during a troubling time in your life.

If an entity does visit you and you are frightened or concerned, you need only to say the words: "*You are only welcome if you walk in the Light of Christ*". Repeat it 3 (three) times. By doing this, you are invoking the Light. Universal Law will protect you; the Creator has promised us this.

All entities are energy forms, and are controlled by Universal Laws. There are dark entities in spirit form, just as there are on the earth plane, as we will explain in more depth in future chapters.

The purpose of us being on the earth plane is for learning. Spirit calls it "earth school". In the spiritual world there are multiple levels or planes of growth which individual entities aspire to reach, the Godhead being on the highest level. Not all entities aspire to reach to the greater heights, some are content wherever they may be, it is their choice.

We each have come down from one of these planes. The reason we return to the earth is for higher learning and growth. We are able to accomplish the lessons at a much faster pace on the earth plane than we can in the spiritual realm. As such we are granted permission to descend to the earth for this learning. Before we arrive here we choose our hair color, the color of our eyes, other physical features, as well as our family, friends, relationships, where we will live, and the lessons we will need while we are here. Then we enter into a sacred contract and then are sent onto the earth plane.

During our time here each one of us has a counsel of approximately 10 – 12 spirit guides & teachers who are with us for various parts of our journey. These numbers can vary from person to person, depending on each individual's purpose here. Their job is to guide and teach us as we fumble through life. After all, none of us are perfect. If we were, we wouldn't be here in the first place! Some guides and teachers also travel with us for the purpose of expanding their own growth. They learn from us. That being understood, there is a rotation and some of them are only with us for a short period of time. When the lessons have been completed they move on, or if we have outgrown a guide they will be replaced. Our levels of growth determine the frequency of when this takes place. Some may stay with us our entire journey from start to finish, others will come and go as needed.

Guides and teachers will often leave you with their name, however not all will, as names are not important in the spirit realm. That again, is a human condition or the humbleness of some guides and teachers prevents them from doing so. They seek no glory for the work they do. Many humans can learn from this.

> *"We are spiritual entities trying to be human. We are not humans trying to be spiritual".*

This is where many faults will lie in ones' understanding. We must learn to recognize this so we do not confuse or misguide ourselves.

When we sleep at night our guides and teachers often come and take us on journeys of higher learning. Before we awaken in the morning they will erase our conscious memories, as these teachings are only meant for us to know when we have returned back to spirit form. These are the higher intelligences that cannot be understood by our human experience. Quite often spirit will attempt to describe concepts and visions but eventually end up saying *"you have no words in your earthly languages to describe what it is we are trying to teach you"*. This is why so many people will have "black" sleeps where they remember nothing; in reality most only dream in the minutes before they awaken in the morning. This is the time when spirit will often give us words of wisdom, visions or guidance for our journey here. We need to pay close attention at this time for clues. Quite often the message will be disguised and may take several visitations prior to us being able to understand what we are being shown. Messages may arrive fragmented and need to be pieced together like a puzzle.

There is no manual in existence that will allow us all the answers to what spirit shows us. Each guide has their own unique identity, their own unique personality and will work with us in a way that may be different from the next guide or teacher. To believe that we can look up a dream or vision in a book is just not accurate, as it is only the interpretation of that author and not that of your guides and teachers.

It is not being implied that one should never read books. What must be done is find the book that speaks to you, asking spirit to let you know if this book is meant for you or not. When visiting the library or bookstore, you will be drawn to a particular subject or writing. When this occurs, hold that book in your hands, send the thought out from your mind asking spirit to confirm if that book is meant for you and then wait. There may be a pause while you focus on the energy or continue to read on. Eventually you will receive a sensation in your solar plexus being one of comfort, indifference or discomfort. This is your sign as to whether you should allow that book's vibration to interfere with your thought processes. Do you feel excitement or intrigued by the information being presented? Ultimately that's what you're after. Did you receive a negative impression such as nausea or disgust? Then put it down, that is not your book; it will guide you down a wrong path.

You must always use common sense and only take from that book the words which speak to your spirit, discarding the rest. Much as this book you are currently reading, if there is something that doesn't speak in a positive way to your spirit then disregard it, you may not be ready at this time to comprehend what is being spoken or it just plainly is not for you. You are the only one who can decide that, because your own spiritual growth is your own responsibility.

Spirit quite often works in symbolism. Your guides or teachers may show you a picture or an image of something. For instance, they may show you an owl. An owl is a very powerful totem animal. The owl has the ability to fly through darkness with great precision, so an interpretation of this vision may be that Spirit has sent you an owl to guide you through a troubling, difficult time. As you can see, they used an animal to symbolically give you a message. It is up to us how we interpret that message. Don't allow anyone to interpret your message for you, as it is "their interpretation" and not necessarily that which Spirit is trying to tell you.

> *Tip:* If you are experiencing a difficult time in life, you can go into prayer and ask Spirit to send you an owl, the owl will help guide you through that dark time. But be careful, owl medicine is very powerful and they are nocturnal, so it may keep you awake at night. Be sure to ask that you are allowed to get your sleep.

Native Americans commonly speak of totem animals often seen during vision quests and in meditation. Some have online resources and books available on this subject.

Why are you seeing totem animals? It may be that you have Native American spirit guides working with you. There are many of them in the spirit realm. Native culture is deeply entwined with Spirit communication and they deserve their due respect both on the earth plane and in the spirit realm. Some of the most powerful spirit guides are Native American. They may come to you as warriors, protectors, teachers and guides. If you work as a healer they may bring powerful medicine through to assist you in your work. Your intent must be pure and not one of ego or greed to be able to attract such a powerful Spirit from the higher realms.

The elders of a tribe carry great wisdom handed down through the generations, there is much to learn from them. The prophecies speak of a time when all shall be as one. Red, yellow, black, brown, white shall put aside their differences and start to receive each other as their fellow man. We will see many starting to blend in marriage in greater numbers than at any time before. There will be a time of greater acceptance and awakening amongst the people.

When being presented with something that you don't understand, ask Spirit to bring it to you again with greater clarity. They will show you 3 different ways, so pay attention, put the pieces together and you will have your answer. If you still don't understand the imagery or dreams presented to you, just focus on the feeling you get when you view these images. Your inner self will tell you how to interpret and understand what is being shown to you.

Meditation is one of the best ways to communicate with Spirit, great wisdom and insight will be brought to you during meditation. It is a time for you to commune with your spirit guides and receive the answers you seek. This is where you will receive clarification for what you are seeking.

Spirit works in very mysterious ways. They tell us to be alert and observe closely what is around us. Many people live their lives with blinders on and don't see or hear what is happening around them. It is important to be open and pay attention to keep from missing sign posts that their guides are placing before them. Be alert, look in the corners, mysterious messages or symbolisms could be there waiting for you. Listen to the whispers of Spirit. Most people cast aside strange occurrences when in reality they need to be paying attention to them.

There is a fine line between what we think it is that Spirit has shown us and what is actually coming from our own mind.

As we become more attuned to walking in the Light, we instinctively begin to learn when Spirit is talking to us. We develop an ability to interpret whether it is our spiritual influences of the Light or our human self that is creating the impressions on our thought processes.

When we become aware of our purpose we are armed with a whole new set of tools for our journey. We can call upon our guides and teachers to help us in certain situations.

They may open a door of opportunity for us and guide us through. Will they map it out perfectly for us? It is unlikely. If we were travelling down our path and should have turned right instead of turning left, we did so of free will and as such we must learn our lessons associated with that decision. This could all be part of our destiny, as we will encounter many difficulties and joys along the way. At the end of the day these are all tools we gather to give us a clearer understanding of the world around us, they assist us in our spiritual and mental growth.

When it is time for us to return back to the Spirit World, we shed the trappings of the earth plane with its material possessions and return with our new found knowledge. Now, what did we do while we were here? Did we commit murder, did we rape, steal from another or abuse someone? Did we give misinformation, act selfishly, lie to others or act in a greedy manner? Did we hide the truth of who we really were or did we waste time baking our brain with drugs and alcohol. How beautiful it would be to be able to say we followed a humanitarian path and assisted others by practicing acts of kindness and compassion.

We have been given free will to do whatever we want, but be aware that universal laws return every injustice. We may think we have gotten away with something, but records are being kept and there will be a price to pay for our actions one day! What kind of energy are you sending out while you are down here?

Chapter 4 • RELIGION

Religion has been ingrained into societies for centuries. For many, ceremonies like marriages and funerals depend upon them. To join an organized religion is by choice. However, it is not necessary as we can learn to commune directly with Spirit ourselves and not be influenced by manmade teachings.

Sacred ground is where you stand to do the work of Spirit. It does not require you to be in a special building or praying in a certain way or buying a special trinket. It does not require you to hand over your paycheck.

Religions that demand tithing only cater to the wealthy, they act out of greed. Poor people can't afford to go to their church, that extra couple of dollars they may have at the end of the week is needed to put food on their table, so in essence they are saying; "we don't want you". That's not very Christian now is it? If done correctly, in a voluntary manner, tithing freely brings rewards to the giver. It will also bring rewards to the organizations that keep that tithing in motion and send it forward to help others. Tithing is not only monetary, if you cannot afford, saying a prayer for another is payment enough.

You create sacred ground wherever it is that you stand to do the work of Spirit and work in the light of truth. Christ walked the earth, he did not contain himself within four walls, he went to the people, he created sacred ground everywhere he stood to speak the word.

One must remember that a preacher's growth can be limited to the four walls in which he or she contains themselves. They may grow beyond that, but quite often they place a block or limitation on their growth by staying within those walls and not venturing forth, as they have set themselves in place to repeat their ministry over and over to the ones that attract to them.

There are many preachers who do have a sincere desire within to help others but are limited to the level of spiritual knowledge they have learned from their teachings. One must be receptive to the higher intelligences to be able to truly guide and assist others on their journey.

Spirit has said;

> *"Religion is like a big wheel and each spoke of that wheel represents each of the different religions. The religions serve a purpose to some because they do eventually lead to the center or hub of that wheel, which is the Godhead".*

This is why Spirit permits even the fraudulent ministers to continue because they are preaching some form of the Word. But do know, the time is coming when all of those not speaking the truth or acting out of hypocrisy, ego and greed will be knocked off the world stages. It's already happening and many more are getting ready to fall, unbeknownst to them and yes, it is coming from above.

People are beginning to awaken and realize that they are disgusted with the dogma and untruths. They go to their churches and discover that some of those they looked up to as their spiritual leaders won't or can't help them through the dark times in their lives, for they possess no desire or knowledge to do so in the first place. As such, many are abandoning that which they used to hold dearly and have started searching for the Light of truth to guide them. This is why so many empty souls are walking around; they are out searching for their soul food.

We are not to condemn or criticize. We are not to teach bigotry and hatred. We are to help others. We are to seek peace and we are to send out compassion. As we do this it shall reach out into the universe. Imagine what we all could do if we filled the entire universe with peace energy! There would be no more wars!

One must question; why are so many wars started and lives lost as a direct result of religious beliefs, when the principles of most religions are supposed to be based on caring for our fellow man? Something sure got lost in the translation.

The Bible says to *be aware of false prophets*. We must always question and be able to think for ourselves. If we are in tune with Spirit we will not be lead in masses by false prophets or those seeking to be the "Great I AM".

It is each individual's choice if they decide to read their version of The Bible. This is not a requirement for many, as the real information of the Spirit is provided from our guides and teachers, as well as our own Spirit, which intrinsically possesses the higher intelligences.

Man is always looking for a more complicated solution but if you tune into spirit and listen with an open heart and pure mind, the answers you seek will be given to you. Become aware of Spirit and work for the betterment of mankind. If you do this, all things will be provided for you and your needs will not be so great.

All things were created for all mankind. Not just for a certain select few to hoard and call their own.

Christ often taught that, we must walk in the white Light of understanding to fulfill our need upon the physical plane.

Joshua is a guide and teacher in spirit who brings great wisdom. He has spoken;

> *"The Creator said go forth and speak my word. He did not say go forth and speak your word!"*

It could not be said any better. Every place of worship in every land should have that statement emblazoned on their walls!

The Godhead is not vengeful, it is loving. When someone tells you that you are going to Hell or will be punished for your deeds they only speak out of ignorance, for many of them do not know beyond their own levels of growth.

There is no physical place as Hell. This is manmade as a method of putting fear into man. If fear is placed into man, the ones placing the fear are in control. If one controls a man's fear, he controls a man's actions and his money. This is a lie perpetrated by certain organized religions that would go so far as to tell you that the devil is speaking these very words to you. This is a very effective method of brainwashing, know the truth! Your own spirit will tell you this truth,

Spirit confirms that there is no place called Hell, they say;

> *"You are in it, you can make your journey Heaven or you can make it Hell, the choice is yours".*

The choice is made by our actions or inactions. So to say you are being sent to a place with the joyous smell of brimstone in the morning and fire boiling cauldrons with some dude in red holding a pitchfork just ain't so. It's up to each individual if they decide to turn up the heat on their own living Hell.

No one could possibly believe that the Creator would ask somebody to murder or commit suicide and take others with them so they can get into Heaven. Those are the words being spoken by men of evil, not the Light of Truth. No one arrives on the earth plane from the Spirit World with that intent. There are some individuals who feel they are entitled to kill others because they feel dishonored by them. There is no honor in murder, nor has any person, in any land, ever been granted that right. All actions of taking another's life are subject to Universal Laws and debts must be paid by all those who defy said laws.

These words are directly from spirit:

"Do you know what the single biggest misinterpretation is in The Bible? It is that Jesus died on the cross for your sins. Jesus did not die on the cross for your sins, he died to show you the way, to show you that there is an afterlife, to show you that there is a Spirit World."

How true, if Jesus died on the cross for our sins then we are free to go and do whatever we want because he already paid for it. What is wrong with that picture?

How misguided so many have been all these years. Universal Laws are put in place to take care of these so called "sins", not our elder brother, He serves a much higher purpose than watching over what we do and judging us for our actions being right or wrong. The Godhead knew all this before the earth plane was populated with souls. The Laws are in place, the Laws are immutable, meaning they cannot be changed by any man or spirit entity.

Is there really any such thing as sin? There is right or wrong. You can covet your neighbor's wife all you want, but be aware that Universal Law will hold you accountable for your actions. Are you going to Hell for it? There's no such place. Universal Law takes care of these things. You must understand what you did and the result it had on others, and realize that you took from another and you hurt others by your actions. You must also be made to realize the power of karma (what you sow, you reap). When we act out of selfishness with little or no regard for our neighbor, we will be made to understand that we are governed by natural laws from which none of us are exempt and the tables "will" be turned one day. That's what it's all about.

There are powerful men of evil who are responsible for creating fear in man pretending to be the ones who will protect you from this evil or fear. They do this solely for their own ego, greed and power. If you do not feed into the manmade fears, you will not become a slave to these men, they will become powerless. It is not only religious leaders being spoken of here. If one tells a big enough lie repeatedly, eventually people will begin to believe it, and these men know that. While many are mesmerized by their belief systems and media overload they become oblivious to what these self proclaimed men of power are doing behind their closed doors, within their secret societies.

We must not lose sight of our own infinite consciousness. Many are beginning to awaken to it. Many times when people are afraid they seek out somebody to follow, to take them by the hand. They quite often run to the ones that caused that fear in the first place.

Man must learn to use the power of their faith and realize these fear mongers are nothing compared to the power of Spiritual Forces of the Light. They will one day be made to pay for what they have done, as there is no defying natural law.

Once we have a better understanding we must wonder if we really need somebody preaching to us, telling us what's right and what's wrong. What we really need is to begin using common sense and act in a civil fashion towards our fellow man. Always remember the Golden Rule; *"Do unto others as you would have them do unto you."* If we always view this statement as positive, we will have managed to manifest that within our lives. It's not complicated. We need spiritual eyes and ears to help us wake up and take control of our own individual destinies. By awakening, one can empower their own being.

Christ was his own trinity, a trinity which is the basis of our existence. This is one of the lessons that was being taught to us; the mind, body and spirit connection. And no, he is not coming back. Spirit has said; *"the Savior will never walk the physical plane again"*. Is he gone? No, he's around us all the time. Christ has spoken; *"When two or more are gathered in my name I am in the midst of them"*. He promised us this and consistent proof has been given repeatedly when he is called upon. There is no need for him to physically walk the earth plane again; he can do much greater work from the spirit side of life.

Though some are comfortable with the group dynamic of weekly gatherings of worship, there are many that are starting to open up to their own spirituality, in that they believe in a higher deity but choose not to follow any specific group or organization. These are the ones that are truly searching their own light of understanding.

We are designed to constantly question and learn, not to take the words of another as gospel, through this we attain greater knowledge and become more receptive to higher intelligences. We have the freedom of independent thinking. It should not be controlled by what others dictate to us. It's not a belief we are to follow; rather knowledge we are to attain. This knowledge becomes installed inside of you. Life doesn't come with a manual, so watch where you put your faith, it can really mess you up.

Chapter 5 • RELATIONSHIPS & SELF

This may sound rather cliché but the best way to describe why people come into our lives is for; a season, a reason or a lifetime. As we progress along life's path we may meet some wonderful people who we care deeply for and then one day it all comes to an abrupt end because of words spoken or actions taken. We find that all of a sudden everything falls apart and we are no longer friends or circumstances have separated us. One must know that everything happens for a reason in the greater scheme of things. We must know that the time has come to move on. Our lessons have been learned with these people and there is nothing further, they must leave now to make room for the next one. This applies to intimate relationships, marriages, as well as friendships and acquaintances.

Unfortunately some cannot handle this truth and act out with violence, jealousy and hatred. There have been many instances throughout history of relationships ending with tragic results because one of the parties involved could not accept the separation.

Rejection and loss are some of the most devastating emotions that trigger dangerous and irrational behavior. Jealousy is a very dangerous negative emotion. Spirit tells us; *"When you are jealous of another, you are merely saying to yourself that person is better than you and this is not true, you are all equal"*. They also go on to say; *"You are in a very high spiritual place when you can send love to your enemies"*. This is excellent advice and besides that, it really screws them up!

You're sending positive energy and they don't know how to receive it because they are wanting to be angry at you. They can't understand where it's coming from.

If you send negative energy you will only fuel the situation and escalate it into an all out battle. We must remember that energy is alive and if we feed it, it continues to grow. What did we learn earlier? We own our actions and we will be repaid tenfold. What's the point; negativity only causes undue stress and illness in our own lives.

Instead of becoming some kind of psychotic bunny boiler, cut the energy, grab your little red wagon, pack up your stuff and head on to your next adventure.

Sometimes we just have to turn the page and walk away. It's not a case of win or lose because there are no winners. It is all a level playing field. Through struggle, there is growth. Clarity of the mind will occur once we work through the struggles in our lives. Crisis and conflict occurs to teach us. If we are learning our lessons, great wisdom is the gift earned. History repeats itself when man doesn't learn the lessons. Unfortunate or tragic events will happen in certain peoples' lives because they are rejecting the lessons being presented.

At the end of the day we must determine, what that person meant to us and the reason why it ended in the way it did. We must take our lessons and walk away with our new found knowledge. It is this knowledge that will guide us in our next relationship.

It is natural that there will be a grieving process involved with the separation of someone who was close to us. We must take time to release the energy, and let go completely. The longer we hold on to this energy, the longer we delay our future meetings, journeys and adventures.

Forgiveness is a form of healing of the soul.

Remember to always keep moving forward and not remain stalled, wallowing in self pity. Self pity is a negative emotion which surrounds our being in darkness; it is a party that nobody wishes to attend. If we stay in this condition, we will find ourselves alone more than we care to be, as we will be pushing away others around us.

Spirit gave a very profound lesson one time;

> *A woman who is abused by her partner may leave that relationship only to find that she enters right back into the same abuse with somebody else and she will continue this cycle until she decides to stand up and say to herself "I refuse to accept this abuse in my life any longer" and then and only then will she be on her path to her own self empowerment, for she has taken control of her own life.*

This is known as the Law of Attraction. One will continue to attract negativity around them until they decide to take control and flip the switch to that which is beneficial in their life.

The Law of Attraction works in both directions; we must be fully aware of this. Light attracts Light and Like attracts Like. If we are negative and trashy in nature, we will only attract that in others. What do we want to be surrounded with?

We are in control of our own conditions in life, no one else is. One must be aware that they are personally responsible for any conditions that they have allowed themselves to be surrounded with.

If we want to initiate change, we must put the Law of Attraction to work for us, it's there and it doesn't cost a thing. It is a very simple law. The Law states what we send out comes back to us (remember the tenfold rule). If we send out kindness to others in our daily routines then we will receive that in return and attract people of the same around us. We will eventually be surrounded by people of a positive nature and those of a negative nature will be repelled by our light.

Opposites may attract but that is temporary, it defies Universal Law. One will always feel inferior to the other. Sure we may want that bad boy or bad girl for that naughty little experience and it may satisfy the rebel in us for awhile but eventually there will be a separation of ways. The other party creates the appeal because of their elusiveness and will usually never commit. Opposites cannot flow together.

We can stay with an opposite all we want, but we must realize what we really seek will just walk on by because we're not in balance with the Law. They'll turn a different corner because we've changed the energy around ourselves and we weren't paying attention, we did not see them.

If one wishes to be miserable and irritating all their life that is their prerogative. It is not going to get us anywhere because we will never be able to attract the positive in our lives. We will only attract more negative, unbalanced and depressed people. Loneliness and illness will come our way as the negative emotions of the world will be attracted to us. Our souls will become darkened if we decide we want to continue to walk down that path, our divinity will be lost.

We cannot be a person who goes around yelling and screaming at others; constantly throwing fits and tantrums and expect to move ahead in life. Nor should we put up with it in life if there is a person around us acting in that manner. We have to slow that crazy train down and get off at the next station to be able to start moving ahead.

We will hopefully wake up one day and realize that there is no glory in trying to make everybody else's life around us as miserable as our own. We will soon discover that these people want nothing to do with us.

We will not learn anything in life because our attitude will refuse to allow the positive to come forward, that which teaches us. We will have placed barriers all around ourselves and be putting up walls that nobody is interested in helping us tear down because they just don't want to be around our energy.

We can remain one of the broken people if we like, or we can crawl out of that space and start repaying our Universal debt. We can change, there's hope....it's our choice. Isn't it time?

We can start by smiling and paying compliments to people, it goes a long way. There is no need to be miserable in life; misery is a condition we place upon ourselves.

Our position in life is of our own doing and no one else's. What we send out comes back, we can choose to blame the world for our problems but one day we will be forced to wake up and realize it was all of our own doing as we obeyed or ignored the unseen laws that govern us. People will begin to see us in the way that we think about ourselves.

Some people we meet along the way are only with us for short periods of time. Quite often it was destined that we were together to help each other along in one form or another. Did it just end softly and we merely parted ways with no unkind words spoken, much like a summer fling filled with fond memories? Or maybe that kind neighbor we chatted with who always made us feel good and expected nothing in return, yet one day we just moved away to never see them again. Was there a reason? Perhaps this person came along to help us through a difficult time in our life? Were they there to guide us around some obstacles we were not seeing or kept running back to? Were we each other's temporary leaning posts?

The purposes of these relationships are not to be merely discarded, as they did bring forward lessons for both parties involved. The lessons may not be on such a grand scale as others we meet along the path, they could have played out on more of a subliminal level, but they do serve their purpose. That purpose usually leaves us with a warm feeling of comfort when we think of them.

Then there are the life-timers, they are our buddies through thick & thin, it doesn't matter what we throw each other's way they will always be there for us and we will always be there for them. These are the ones that never leave our side. They expect nothing of us and we expect nothing of them but we are destined to be a beacon to one another. Many times we may take these people for granted and we shouldn't, because it's not until they're gone that we may realize what they really meant to us.

We know who these people are in our lives because we feel a connection between our spirit energies. There is a bond that is unbreakable, even if it is a love/hate relationship; because ultimately deep down inside we have a caring connection for the welfare of each other. We may not even speak for months or years on end, and then suddenly we meet again and pick right up where we left off, as if there had been no separation at all.

Do know that we are most likely connected with these people on the spirit side of life, as there is a soul connection. We feel it within; we know who these people are around us. No matter what the situation or purpose of other individuals we've met along the path served, we must recognize what it means to us. What am I supposed to take from this? What lessons have I learned? Can I walk away with my head held high? The relationships we encounter are all lessons along the way. So we must take the lessons and use them as tools to forge meaningful relationships in our future. Whether it is in business or our personal lives; never burn a bridge that we may have to walk across again one day.

Quite often when we feel anger towards another, it is best to write the letter and never send it. It allows us to release our emotions and not close the door. Once we have slept on it for a night, we should go back and read it again. In most instances, we will realize that we were glad it never went.

If we want to improve our quality of life we must begin with ourselves. We must put the Law of Attraction to work in our everyday life and watch what happens, we will be pleasantly surprised. It doesn't matter how badly we may have acted in the past, we can always change. True change is positive, hold no fear.

Many times we may find people around us who feel qualified to offer us their opinion on matters that affect our lives. Feel free to listen to them, but by no means do we need to accept the words they are speaking. Realistically, it is what "they" would do; it is not necessarily what is good for us. We should choose the words spoken that are of interest to us and discard the rest.

People must make their own decisions. We can tell some one "you should do this" but it will only trigger their defenses. One is better suited to making the suggestion instead. "Have you thought of maybe trying it this way?"

There is nothing we can do to change anything done in our past. Sometimes we may feel ashamed about choices we have made in life and others will attempt to make us feel badly about ourselves. We must never allow anyone to do this. When we take control of the situation, then we remove their power. We do this by taking responsibility for our actions.

At times the mind needs to discover things for itself. This self discovery opens new pathways of learning. We have our own ability to find solutions to problems in our lives, we just need to listen to our higher selves--we intrinsically know this. This explains why we often go on the defensive if we feel someone is trying to interfere with us. Once we learn to apply the relationship lessons we have been taught from our different encounters, we can work towards building more meaningful relationships and friendships in our lives.

We are all creatures of nature and touch is very important to us; whether it is physical human touch or something that touches our heart. This emotion is important to our earthly being. It makes us feel wanted and gives us a sense of belonging.

There are many who believe that they must say or hear the words "I love you", when involved in a relationship or friendship. However, this is not always necessary, as some individuals do not wear this emotion on the outside. These are merely words, the reality being, this is an emotion that comes from the heart. It is an energy that is felt between individuals, which does not even require words. One should not be discouraged if they do not hear these words from another, simply look into their eyes to know the truth. It scares the heck out of some people when they hear those words but deep down it has a place.

> The most important lesson to learn about relationships remains in the fact that; *we cannot give that which we do not possess ourselves.*

If we have not learned how to love ourselves, there is no way possible that we can love another. Our relationships will continuously fail because we have not learned this lesson in life and only seek to have another fulfill it for us. This is not how it is meant to be.

Many people enter into relationships with the expectation of "this is the one". They place all their emphasis on the fact that this "new" person will change them. Change comes from within, not from without. Another person cannot do this for us; it is something we must accomplish on our own.

If we are serious about having a committed relationship, we need to change the energy around ourselves. When one loves self they are fully confident in who they are and comfortable within their own body. They have an air of confidence in their being. This is a powerful tool within the Law of Attraction, as many others will feel and see this in our energy and will gravitate towards us. It will make us more desirable to others, as they will seek to be with and around us. The unseen laws will be at work and we will attract another who is of equal. This is a solid path that we can place ourselves upon and bring that which we may seek.

Some people are filled with self loathing within themselves. They truly despise their own being from within. These thoughts may be related to deeds done in their past, conditions they have placed upon themselves, or they think they're not pretty enough or have a certain style, wealth or position in life. Those are all shallow earthly conditions that one must release from within.

We are not to stand in judgement before others. Man places too much emphasis on the condition of the physical form and not enough emphasis on the condition of the spirit within. It is the spirit within that is the true powerhouse of our well being. The spirit within is what will bring us toward that which we desire.

We must learn to separate the physical from the spiritual and then learn how to blend these into one cohesive unit, allowing us to live in harmony within ourselves. When we accomplish this, we achieve greatness within. The conditions that enslave ones' being will be lifted, as they will have learned how to attune to their own higher self.

Our spirit resides on both sides of the veil. The spirit residing within our earthly vessel is but a portion of our greater spirit body which is still residing on the higher side of life (the Spirit side). Only a portion of our spirit body is sent down to the earth plane for our journey, this is our connection to our greater spirit form on the other side.

Do not inflict damage to our spirit is the lesson here, we must learn how to balance and harmonize within. We must remember that the day will come when we will be fully reunited with our heavenly spirit vessel.

As we learned earlier, we possess two vessels, the ethereal or spirit body and the material or physical body. We must care for both and take care not to pay too much creed to the physical. This is not to say that we should let our physical body go, it is to understand that one should create a balance. This is a valuable lesson in spiritual enlightenment.

The lessons from the Universe are tools that are free, they are there for all to use. We just need to reach out and grab ours and start applying it within. Every one is different, so all courses are different. No two conditions are the same. Spirit entities are as unique as human entities and each possess their own set of characteristics. One must learn to harmonize within and balance the spiritual and physical.

When we stand back and look at the simple lessons that spirit presents to us, we begin to realize that it is not that complicated. We can have that which we desire, and the way to get there is to retrain our way of thinking and our way of being. When we retrain our processes of thought and action we put the universe at our doorstep. This is the starting grounds where one launches from to accomplish all of the other goals in life.

We tend to focus on what worries us and often we blow those worries out of proportion, ignoring all the good things around us. Worry energy is wasted energy.

People often create unnecessary worry energy in their minds, whether it is worry about a child, money, work, relations, etc., they play the thought over and over in their mind. They create a repetitive thought process, only to discover that what they are so worried about never occurs. What wasted energy! We should send this energy off as soon as it creates in your mind. It is not needed, as it will only manifest itself into negative conditions around us and zap the good energy that we could be better directing elsewhere. Everything begins from within. We must fix ourselves first and then we can go forward to accomplish whatever our heart desires.

When we learn how to commune within ourselves, greater lessons will start flooding our way. The lessons are all good, although it may not seem like it at the time. They are meant to move us forward in life. Without this learning, there is no growth within.

If a lesson is repeated that means we did not get it the first time, so we must step back and observe what we missed.

Our spirit guides will keep bringing our lessons back to us until we get them right, it's their job to do so, per our spiritual contract with them.

If we discover that our life is constantly going around in a circle like a dog chasing its tail, then we must stop and take a serious look at what could be causing this to occur.

Our guides are repeating our lessons. What is it that we are doing wrong? We have to figure out the answer, fix it and our guides will remove the lesson allowing us to continue on our journey. This may seem harsh if they are tough lessons we are going through, but when we finally become aware of the reasoning, we can recognize why it is necessary.

If we are having difficulty figuring out what our lesson is, then we need to go into meditation and focus on it, asking our guides and teachers to reveal it to us. We request them to bring the lesson to the surface so we may correct it. They will do it. We must start paying close attention to what we are shown over the next short period of time.

When all is revealed to us, we can begin to repair it. This is a very important step, as one cannot move forward if they are running around in circles. We must correct it so we can move ahead once again. Some people spend their entire earthly lives in one big circle, as they have not comprehended this aspect of their existence while on the earth plane.

We cannot experience growth without learning. When we stop learning, we stop growing.

When one says "I already know all that", that person allows their ego to place obstacles on their path and they immediately stop growing. No learning, no growth. We are never to stop learning on the earth side or when we return to the spirit side.

We must learn to become the master of our own emotions, desires and passions. When we learn how to master these conditions, we can dictate our purpose and position on this earthly plane. We become in control of our own destiny. We can walk in confidence with our head held high, knowing we are on the right path. We must be that which our own spirit is pushing us towards, if we let it, it will guide us.

What may come across as negative on this plane may not be on the spirit side. Everything happens for a reason. Whether our negative condition involves illness or other lessons we need, we must realize that all things do serve their purpose. Until one truly understands what the purpose is, we may resist or lash out in anger with some of these negative conditions, especially if we continuously hold on to them. Acceptance is a starting ground to releasing such conditions.

Strong relationships with our own self and those around us build a strong foundation for our advancement into our future. We can be depressed about what has gone wrong in our lives or we can focus on everything that is right.

Life is a series of events. It is so easy to allow our spirits to be crushed by setbacks. If we rejoice in the smaller accomplishments, we keep moving forward in a more positive direction. We need to release the old energy in our lives, it weights us down and prohibits our growth.

When change comes it may be forced upon us in a harsh way. Whether we have been fired from a job through a chain of events that seems to be no fault of our own, or maybe the change came with the ending of a relationship, we should not look at it as a tragic event in our life. The doom and gloom feeling that inevitably comes with the occurrence of that event should not be magnified by allowing ourselves to fall into a state of depression and panic.

Nature has a way of pushing us when we won't make the moves ourselves. We need to give death to the old situation as fast as we can and not allow it to control our life. Do not waste it seeking vengeance. That door closed for a reason. That reason is because we are supposed to move on to the next phase of our blueprint.

We must not allow fear on our path. When one door closes, the next one opens. Compliance with natural law states we must close the old door to have the ability to open the next. We must have faith that something new is waiting right around the corner for us. This doesn't mean we get to just sit on our butts and wait for it, we must start venturing forward in the new energy, keeping it positive to allow that magnification to build.

Through our journeys and encounters with others in life, sometimes we made mistakes and we allowed our memory to punish us long after. We need to release these memories to free our hearts. It is no longer relevant, we can't fix the past, we can only work towards a brighter future. The future will always give us a chance.

There's a reason if somebody from our past doesn't make it to our future. Let that energy go and move forward.

Chapter 6 • SPIRIT & SEX

Many questions start to unfold as people become attuned to a spiritual presence in their life.

One major question people timidly ask; "*Is spirit watching when we have sex?*" As a matter of fact, yes, they are watching you and reporting and grading you. Your performance goes on your spiritual report card at the end of your journey. But seriously; not to traumatize and send people scrambling to become born again virgins – they are not watching. Sexual organs have been built into the human body by design. Male and Female sexual organs are not solely for the purposes of waste disposal and breeding. They are built in to assist the body's natural chemical processes, showing us that the respective organs serve a healing purpose in the body.

Humans regard sex much differently than does Spirit. Some are ashamed of it and some really don't care if the entire world is watching them. There's a wide open field of extremes here. Sexual energy relates to inner human desires and wanton lusts, which are conditions that do not exist in the spirit realm. This is an earthly condition.

People often confuse the very high loving energy of Spirit with that of lust. One may work with a mentor, spiritual leader, healer or medium to seek their guidance in life and quite often develop an attraction to them. They confuse the loving energy that Spirit brings forth during the healing process with an overwhelming desire to have sex with that individual and will often attempt to pursue it. This person may have brought the individual great comfort and a sense of caring, which can be confused by the individual. It is equally important for all parties concerned, especially if you are the Light worker. Do not cross that line, you are risking your gifts, and you would be abusing your privilege in life. You must teach yourself and your client to deal with that energy.

This does not mean that you cannot work on a spiritual level with someone you are having relations with, there are no rules prohibiting that, however, you may not abuse any perceived positions of control or authority, as you will have seriously fallen out of compliance with Universal Law and will become subject to those laws.

When one decides to have relations in life is their prerogative. There are no rules in place. You do not have to wait for a specific time. It is of one's own doing and free-will. Though Spirit is not watching over you when you have sex, it does not mean that you can have a free for all. You are still bound by Universal Law. There are manmade laws and there are spiritual laws and they must be followed or you will be subjected to the repercussions involved with those laws.

Energy is energy, no matter where or how it gets created. All energy goes into the universe. We are never to abuse another, take from another or cause harm to another. We will pay the price if we defy this. As common sense dictates, everything must be mutually agreed upon by all parties concerned.

We must also be aware not to abuse self. Many individuals that follow the path of obsessive sex often find their lives empty and shallow. They cannot form meaningful relationships in their lives because they have not learned to love themselves. To compensate for their emptiness within, they act in an outward fashion and make themselves available to anybody that is willing, wandering the streets for someone to take them home. We must be aware that when we do this we are creating this energy around ourselves.

Spirit has spoken:

> *"Nobody wants the girl in town that everybody has been with. They want the girl that nobody has been with."*

So you see, if we are seeking to have a meaningful relationship in life, it would be appropriate to take heed of these words, as this energy will radiate from your being and others will feel it around you. This applies to men as well as women. It doesn't matter if we are gay/lesbian or heterosexual; the same rules apply to all. If we wish to attract a loving partner in life, it is best to retain a little mystery of ones' self. We create an allure that others will desire in us.

Once we understand how to stay balanced with our spiritual self we will have a greater respect for ourselves and others.

We will learn how the Laws of Attraction work and how to bring into being that which we desire.

We can be very spiritual people and still enjoy that which life has to offer. We are not expected to become prudes.

Play safe, respect other's boundaries and have fun!

Chapter 7 • THE TWO SPIRITED

This is a Native American expression used to describe Gays and Lesbians. First off, political correctness; Lesbian is the term used to describe two-spirited women and Gay is a term used to describe two-spirited men. Two-Spirited is non-gender specific, it refers to an individual encompassing both the masculine and feminine energies within one vessel.

It is a gift from above if you were permitted to come down here and be two-spirited while you walk the earth plane. Be thankful for what has been granted to you. One does not choose to be gay or lesbian after they get here, it is not a lifestyle choice or a phase that one goes through. It is who you are.

Those who speak out against the two-spirited bring forward falsehoods, calling them immoral while they are spreading their bigotry and hatred. They speak from a place of ignorance. They are of a lower vibration, which has not yet reached the levels of intelligence and growth to see beyond their own prejudice. None of these people were given the right to judge, yet they judge with such ignorance. Being two-spirited is not a choice, being prejudiced is. It makes one wonder what these objectors are afraid of.

The Bible was redesigned by man to suit the individuals rewriting it. Spirit brought to light a very important lesson one day to prove that The Bible was rewritten by man -- they said; *"Go and read James Chapter 6"*. Take some time to go now and read it for yourself. You will see the lesson they were bringing.

To say that the Creator is either male or female would be placing limitations upon the divine source of all creation and we cannot do that.

It was asked of Spirit if the Godhead possesses masculine and feminine energies. Their response was: *"There is neither a masculine or feminine, there is no gender."*

The Godhead is an energy source which spirit describes as:

> *"A light so bright it would blind a mere human. Beams of light come out of this energy source and connect to your crown chakras."*

(The crown chakra is located at the top of your head.)

The Two-Spirited are what one may call the third sex. In Spirit there is no differentiation of masculine or feminine, hetero, gay or lesbian, this is a human condition.

You don't need science to tell you that mens' and womens' thought processes are entirely different from each other. Men do not think or see things the same way that women do. Those who are two-spirited possess the duality and encompass both energies, they are able to see situations from both points of view. What a wonderful gift to possess! Know that you are indeed truly blessed!

Why the third sex? Males have always thought of themselves as the dominant ones over the females on the earth plane. If we are all made in the Creator's likeness then that means we are all to be equal, so how can one sex dominate the other? This belief conflicts with the balance of nature.

Both heterosexual males and females possess the opposite gender's energy within their bodies but they have their own gender more dominant than the other. Heterosexuals possess this duality but it is in more minute traces – we all possess each other's physical chemical makeup being that men have estrogen in their bodies and women have testosterone. It is in a natural balance.

In nature, males possess a masculine energy and females possess a feminine energy, so this means that the two-spirited must possess the polarities of both these energies to create that common ground between the two sexes. Nature must always be in balance or it would cease to exist. Everything in nature must be complete, it forms a trinity, and one could call this a completion of that trinity.

The two-spirited are closer to our original ethereal existence encompassing both of these energies. This does not mean the two-spirited are better, we are all equal. It means they have the ability to tap into both the masculine and feminine divine energies as one, as they possess a more even balance of each energy; understand this ability and you will find that you are able to tap into a higher vibration.

If you are two-spirited, learn to harness this energy and you will see great possibilities come forward in your life. You will begin to view things from a different perspective. Look beyond and in all directions, you will see your blueprint in a whole new light.

Being two-spirited is not something you can fake, you are born that way. And it is definitely not something you can "cure" what a pathetic statement that is. There are groups of people who actually believe they can cure the two-spirited. It makes one wonder which universe these people come from. They believe they have the ability to take away a gift that was granted by the Creator, so in reality they are positioning themselves above God. These people must think very highly of themselves to be able to undo God's work.

For those that follow The Bible as the authentic Word of God, pay attention to what is truly being said. In the first couple of chapters in the book of Genesis, we are told of the two-spirited...

In the story of the creation of Adam and Eve; Adam was placed in the garden first and then Eve was created from his rib. The feminine came out of the masculine. We are being told that his body contained the duality. The question was asked of Spirit how the creation of man came to be, this is their response:

> *"The atom split into who you know as Adam and his energy split into Eve and the energy manifested forth. "*

It was further asked if this is representative of the masculine/feminine duality of our spiritual existence and their response was *"yes"*. This means that we all come from a life form that encompasses both energies in the same spiritual body.

Earthly bodies, whether they be man or woman (gay/lesbian or straight) embody both energies within their spirit. The two spirited are just more attuned to the dual energies within the same vessel and have a more equal balance of both energies.

> It was further asked of Spirit if Adam reincarnated multiple times, their response was; *"the masculine only reincarnated one time, the feminine went on to many incarnations."*

One must open their eyes and observe what they're missing. The Bible tells us that we are all created from a two-spirited life form. Remember, many individuals speak their own word and not that of our Creation. When they read The Bible they read selectively, ignoring what they do not wish to accept in life.

The truth is we are all created from a life form that encompasses both energies. Some evolve into masculine or feminine beings and some remain two-spirited. If we decide to go out and speak with prejudice against the two-spirited, we are merely speaking with prejudice against our own creation. As these individuals spread their hatred, they need to be reminded that their judgement day will come;

they are only foolishly sending negative energy at themselves. Hatred and prejudice does not come from a God of unconditional love.

There is a very important message being sent here to all of the two-spirited people who have been lied to by their religious leaders or peers. Know that you are special and uniquely made, you are a gift from the Creator, who does not make mistakes. Do not accept the negative words being spoken to you or any negative conditions placed upon you. If it is safe to do so, leave the situation that imprisons you and seek your truth. The truth will set your spirit free and the burdens will be released from the weight that has been placed upon you.

You have been granted the gift of being able to walk the earth plane as one who is two-spirited, don't hide your gift, bring it forward so you can fulfill what you are called to do while you are here. You must be careful though to make sure you are safe before doing so. Ask Spirit in prayer for wisdom and protection and it will be granted to you, but pay attention and follow their guidance.

We only become prisoners if we allow another to imprison us. No one has the right to hold control over another, no matter what the situation is. If you choose to remain in that which enslaves you, then you only have yourself to blame. You have free will, move to another town, city, country whatever is required to be free. Ask spirit to lay out a path for you, pay attention, be smart and place no fear on that path.

time. There is no alternative to this. The only appropriate action is to stand back and be supportive.

Those who choose to remain closeted throughout their life and not speak their truth do so by their own choice, but they must look inside. Why are you afraid? One is not to live their life wearing a mask. We are intended to walk only one path at a time. This is a major stress that one would carry through life, living in fear of being discovered. In some cases, this fear can manifest and one's own spirit can cause the individual to accidentally reveal themselves, realizing after the fact that you were most likely in a glass closet and most people around you already knew, or didn't really care. It is a very good way to find out who your real friends are; they are the ones who will stay standing beside you.

If you are in a situation where you feel unsafe, most definitely wait. You will know when the time is right. There are many people who bully or torment those that are different than them, usually because of their own ignorance or fear.

Watch those that "protest" too much, for the most outspoken generally do so out of some form of guilt – don't interact with these people, they're not worth wasting your energy on. It is important to rise above these people and not engage in the negative energy they are spreading. These people are on a much lower vibration and lower universal knowledge/intelligence, causing them to act this way.

The younger you are the worse it can seem. It is very difficult for a teenager to come out. Too many have ended up committing suicide afterwards because they cannot handle the constant bullying and negativity. If you are in this situation, work towards fixing it, seek out an individual that can help guide you through and remove you from that situation. You do not need to stay in a negative environment, find a safe haven and go there. There are other places to go, there are other alternatives, you are not stuck where you are; we always have a choice. There are many people who will stand beside you because they are just like you or they understand and are willing to assist you— seek them out.

If you are younger and know that you have been born gay or lesbian and feel a desire to let everybody know, you would be very wise to analyze the situation before making such a bold move. Determine who the people are around you and how they will respond. If you know your parents and family members or your school will not support you then it may not be the right time for you. Have patience and reveal your inner truth at a later date in time (this can be years later), when you feel it is safer. There are no set timelines for your announcement. So be safe, be patient, you will know inside when the time is right to move ahead. Don't be foolish in your decisions, think them through and speak with those you know you can trust—you are not alone, there is somebody somewhere to assist you, whether it is a support group, friend, or phone line, find them and be safe.

There is a very impressive list of two-spirited individuals who have risen to stardom and achieved greatness in their lives.

There is a certain international singing sensation who presented a whole lot of *Faith* to the world. His debut solo album became one of the best selling albums of all time, staying on the Billboard charts for over 80 weeks. This album went on to top the British, American, Canadian and Dutch charts. It also achieved multi-platinum status in the U.S. and UK. When one listens, you can sense a divine inspiration in his music, you can hear it in the vibration; a vibration that appeals to both genders with the same raw compassion. He has created a body of work which shall remain legendary.

As a performer, being two-spirited enables one to tap into both the masculine and feminine energies and create the lyrics and melodies that appeal to both sexes; you would be one who sees both sides.

When your mission in life is divinely inspired there is nothing that can stop it outside of yourself. Your rise will occur very rapidly. This is ones' destiny.

Freddie Mercury's passing undoubtedly changed the musical landscape. He is another shining star that will always remain legendary with his grandly flamboyant performances that also worked magic across the genders. Though he has gone back to the spirit realm, his music and energy lives on. He cemented a place in history during his short time with us. His creative genius may have been cut short, but we are still honored to have been witness to his celebrity.

Whether they are female or male, there are many artists, musicians, talk show hosts, actors and writers which have reached international celebrity status. Famous two-spirited people have existed throughout time and they always will. They serve as shining examples to the two-spirited communities, of the heights which can be attained, when one taps into their God-given gifts and reaches for what is rightfully theirs.

Everyone has something deep within their soul that is just waiting to come forward, you can feel it within you, yet we hesitate to enter the unknown. When we are fearful we sometimes place obstacles in our own path. Bring forward that for which you are destined. We're not all rock stars or actors, perhaps yours is a gift of healing or your purpose is a humanitarian one, to serve in the welfare and betterment of others, whatever your calling is, let it shine.

THE TRANSGENDERED

Before we leave this subject, we must address the transgendered communities. Transgendered is also not a choice made in life. A spirit is placed in a body of which the energies are not in balance with nature, they may be a masculine energy in a feminine body or vice versa.

It is on both a physical and psychological level, the individual is born with the thought processes and energy of the opposite gender.

Those that are transgendered know it at a very early age, some as early as 18 months. Often those around them will call it a "phase" they are going through but the individuals themselves know something is unique about them. Many have attempted suicide because they feel that they are not normal and they feel alone. There is a lot of confusion involved when one discovers that their mind and energy is not what their body represents.

The only way to make things right in their world is to transition. Once this transition takes place, the individual is reborn and feels that everything is now proper in their world. It ends that suffering.

Many transgendered individuals are old souls. They bring great lessons to those around them, lessons in tolerance and caring. They are very brave individuals who take ownership of their being. They are not afraid to be who they are and do not hide from their light. It's very difficult for an outsider to understand the internal strength required to make such a bold move in ones' life.

We can learn from the lessons they bring to us. Instead of judging these individuals, we should take note of the power within them. We live in such a racist, hate filled world, yet these souls bravely present their light for all to see.

It is up to the individual to find which course of alignment or path they wish to follow, usually they will follow that which is strongest within their spirit. There is no right or wrong answer, it's all about their own desire within and what makes them whole. No man should stand in judgement for they cannot even begin to understand the turmoil within. Those that are transgendered have not been forsaken; you are all children of the Creator, who loves all equally. This is your path.

The lessons learned are for your growth and those around you, just as the hetero, gay, lesbian or bi worlds exist so does yours. You are all part of the community and the choices you make are yours, follow your heart, confer with your guides in meditation and seek the answers to which will free any weight which you have placed upon your soul.

We all ascend back to the heavens when it is our time, no one is exempt. There is no right or wrong decision to be made. Do as your spirit speaks to you, but remember to be safe in your decisions.

Ones' sexuality is never superior to another's. We all walk separate paths and serve different purposes while down here. The different sexual orientations are a valuable lesson in tolerance and understanding.

Chapter 8 • THE GREAT BALANCING ACT

There are no chemical solutions to a spiritual problem.

When one chooses to hide from troubling issues in their life by masking it with pharmaceuticals, drugs, alcohol, food, sex, or other addictions, that person has only managed to become a slave to that chemical or behavior. People quite often don't know where to look to find a solution to that which troubles them, nor do some even care to.

One may go through life placing countless limitations and blocks on their own spiritual growth by creating excuses for their inability to move forward.

Every addiction has its own story; physical appearance, sexual abuse, loss of a loved one, parental alcoholism, broken lives...so many occurrences that can lead one down a path of denial.

People place so many conditions and fears on themselves, effectively blocking them from moving forward in life. They slam on the brakes and life just seems to stop dead for them. They have built walls and enslaved themselves to that which prevents them from becoming what they were meant to be. They have dimmed their light and darkened their divinity within.

If you remove your fears and tear down those walls, you will release that which is weighing you down and enslaving you, allowing you to move forward in life. It will reignite your divinity and allow it to burn brightly once again. You serve no purpose to yourself or to others when you place these conditions upon yourself. If you have done this, it is time to wake up; you're failing your mission in life.

Everything we encounter in life is a lesson. Did you choose that path before you came here? Who were you in a previous life? Is this your repayment to the universe for past deeds? Is it a lesson needed? We don't know the answers to these questions while here. Unfortunate incidences happen in life, we are intertwined with all different vibrational levels of growth around us each day. In any case we must learn to rise above it. We must learn to keep ourselves protected and walking in the Light to which we have been destined.

When one places themselves in a lower vibration, meaning they sink into depression or darkness, they have opened up the gateways to dark entities. There are dark forces in the unseen world, they have not gone through the Light and they seek to impinge upon others on the physical plane, to interfere with their energy. They regard these energy disruptions and instilling fear as badges of honor in their dark realm.

These dark entities walk the veil between the spirit world and the physical world. Spirit has indicated that they do have their own realm. They prey upon the weak. When you have placed darkness and depression upon yourself, constantly medicating yourself with pharmaceuticals, drugs or alcohol, you become weak, you become a target for them.

Is this meant to scare you? In a way, yes! It's a wake up call to realize that we must walk in a perfect white light of protection every moment of our earthly existence. We must walk the talk.

Do not confuse these dark entities with the devil. There is no such thing as the devil. That is something that is made up by organized religions for control. These are entities of a lower vibration, which are scared to go through the Light. They are welcome to go through when they pass into spirit but they are fearful of it, so they choose to walk the veil between. They are at a lower vibration than a Light walker.

There are many documented cases of people encountering evil from unseen forces in their lives. You must always remember that darkness is merely the absence of light. If you feel the presence of a dark entity, just say out loud;

> "*In the name of the Heavenly Father, I command you to leave immediately*"

> Repeat it three times, forcefully. They will scatter, they fear the light.

Dark entities can bring physical harm if you allow it. They may attempt to control you, just do not permit it. You've seen it in the news; some guy will say the voices in his head told him to commit the crime. Some of the time these are real voices they are hearing (not always the case though, sometimes they are lying to get away with their deed). They have become weak and allowed the darkness to rule them. Don't let anybody ever tell you it is the work of the devil, they do not speak the truth to you.

Universal Law protects us when we use the tools given to us. Command the power of the Light to work for you. You cannot allow fear in your life, fear feeds the energy.

If you have been paying attention and you continuously walk in the white light of protection, you will have never placed yourself in this position to begin with. You will always be safe and protected, you will become untouchable to darkness. This has a dual effect, as it will keep your moods elevated and you will start to find your happiness in life.

The Creator has promised to protect us, we will not be forsaken, but we must ask for this protection and we must seek to walk in that perfect Light. This is Universal Law. Light attracts Light, Like attracts Like. We must constantly ask to be surrounded in this white light of protection. Dark entities fear the Light, they fear the Godhead, and so if you remain surrounded in that Light you will never be concerned about being impeded by such dark forces.

Light is forever powerful. Darkness is merely the absence of light. When night time comes it is not darkness that overpowers, it is a lack of sunlight. When the light reappears at dawn, it overpowers the darkness. The exact same relationship can be applied to entities of Light and entities of darkness. Introduce Light and the darkness is gone.

Everything must always be in balance. We must have a greater understanding to be able to interpret how we see light and dark. If we have fallen into a dark place, we will be presented a ladder. We can call this a ladder of darkness or a ladder of light; how we interpret this depends on which side of the light we are looking at it. Once we begin to climb this ladder, we will become a more enlightened and balanced individual. We have risen above and witnessed both sides. We achieve a greater understanding.

Be careful not to misinterpret the words being spoken. It is not being said that you absolutely must fall into a dark place to be enlightened, but rather to understand if you have allowed yourself to fall, use this as an opportunity to learn. The more difficult the lessons of life, the more advanced the learning. Through these, greater knowledge is obtained.

Who are the best teachers in life? They are not the person who read about it from a textbook in a classroom, but rather those who walked the path, those who lived the experience. They are authentic teachers who can teach others first hand and guide them through the darkness. They can tell you how they made it back to the light. This is how one places their beacon on a hill to guide others. Take the lessons learned, get up, dust yourself off and keep moving forward.

You may think that's easier said than done. Of course it is. Anything worthwhile doesn't come easy and nothing is free in life. There are tools that can be used to get you there and get you there quickly.

Impatience is a common human trait. The trip always seems so long to get there, and is so much shorter on the way home, yet it is the same distance. The anxiety brought on by waiting is the most difficult part; yet easily cured with patience.

There are many who want what they can't have and can't deal with what they've already got. Many of these same individuals need to be thankful for their lessons received both good and bad. We are always looking for quick fixes but there are no shortcuts. There is no magic pill. We must train ourselves to understand the value of the wait. If you find yourself in that position, there are some tools to help you get through.

THE BALLOONS

You were taught earlier that we all have guides and teachers while on our journey here. They can perform many important tasks, including healing and assisting in our spiritual growth.

Here is a technique in its simplest form to be able to communicate with your guides and teachers. Find a quiet area. You are going to do a mini meditation. This is very quick and only takes a minute or two.

Sit upright comfortably with your feet flat on the floor. Place your hands on your lap with your palms facing up. Close your eyes. Now visualize that you are holding a string in your hand and at the end of that string is a pink balloon floating above you. Now take whatever the problem or condition is that troubles you and place it inside of this pink balloon. It can be anything (a house, car, money, person, job, relationship etc). Visualize this item inside of the pink balloon. Now take your other hand and visualize yourself cutting the string. Watch the balloon as it floats above you up into the universe. It will get smaller and smaller until you can no longer see it. Now wait and feel the energy that returns to you and accept the energy. It is a healing vibration.

You can repeat this as many times a day as you wish. You can also change what you place inside the balloon each time.

A lot of people may think this exercise is ridiculous or silly, but it has a lot of merit. Your Spirit guides and teachers were observing you every step of the way. What you have done is taken your condition and placed it inside this balloon so your spirit guides could remove it from you because you can no longer handle it. You are releasing it. Your guides watch you do it.

Most consider pink to be a color associated with perfect love, so you have sent your problem off with love, which is a positive vibration. You have just changed the vibration of that condition from negative to positive. You have released the condition and allowed the Universe to take care of it for you.

You must be patient and allow Spirit time to work through the issue you gave them. You will be pleasantly surprised to learn that in a short period of time your problem is usually solved. An answer will be brought to you or a troubling condition lifted. Pay attention to what happens in your life after allowing Spirit to take control. You don't want to miss out on your solution. Spirit will provide you with proof of their existence and their desire for your highest good.

One must be careful though, you cannot place anything of ego or greed inside of that balloon for it will not be answered. When this happens we must realize that our guides have placed a block on what we asked for. It may disappoint us at the time but at a later date we will realize that it was done for a reason. We must be careful what we wish for. We may have asked for something only to realize a short period of time later "*I am glad that never happened*". We must realize our guides are always, without exception, looking out for what is best for us.

Please do not start releasing real balloons into the atmosphere. This is not necessary, what you were just taught is done through the mind's eye; it is not with a physical material item. The environment is harmed every time balloons are released. If you release a balloon, it has to land somewhere and when it does animals may consume the rubber and choke on it or birds may become entangled in the strings. Please use common sense and do not pollute the earth and endanger wildlife.

"I asked the Creator for something and my hands were left empty." It is possible there is something even greater being prepared for us. It all amounts to the amount of faith we have that the best will be done for us, to the highest of good of all involved.

Now we must also be very careful what we ask for. Spirit has a very keen sense of humor. We may ask for something and it gets delivered. Then we're standing there thinking *"that's not what I meant"* and Spirit would respond *"that's what you asked for"*. The expression *"be careful what you wish for"* is a very powerful statement!

When we ask something of spirit, we must be very specific, right down to the finest detail, for if we don't, we will just get what we asked for. Did you ask for "a man who's blonde with a tan"? Did you remember to make sure that he can support himself, he's not bringing a ton of baggage, he's good natured and he's mentally balanced? Do you see the point? Be specific.

Once you ask for something, do not change it because you may confuse your guides. They've already gone to work for you assisting with your request. Be smart and think before you ask. More importantly; *be careful what you wish for!*

Do you need help with paying bills, buying groceries or covering rent? Put it in the balloon. The majority of people think that you cannot ask the Creator or Spirit for money. They are so wrong. Spirit knows we live in a material world and require material goods. As long as we do not ask out of greed it will be granted. As long as we are responsible with it once we receive it, it will be granted repeatedly. When one becomes attuned to Spirit, their needs will not be so great.

You can send the thought out; *"Spirit, I need help paying this bill, please bring me a solution so I may take care of it."* Remember our previous lesson, *"thought is energy"* you created the energy and have sent it into the universe, the energy is yours, it will be returned to you.

We must always remember to be grateful and give thanks to Spirit, when our request has been granted. We must be thankful if it is not delivered as well. It is not only good manners, but it sends a message to Spirit that you are ready for more. You've cut the energy of your old condition; it has been solved, and now you are free to move forward. Always give thanks.

When we do receive our blessings they don't just fall out of the sky. They will be presented to us in many ways, so pay attention and realize where the ultimate source is from. You may ask for help buying food or paying bills and it may present itself with additional work, or an unexpected windfall. It will be brought to us in some way...don't miss out when the opportunity presents itself. If you reject what is presented, then Spirit will remove it and you will miss the blessing. They will not waste their time if you continually refuse what is presented, so be aware in how you are receiving your gifts.

The balloons are not just about material possessions. They are also used for healing oneself or another. Quite often one carries conditions in their life that manifest into all kinds of illnesses of the body and mind. We may be carrying something from childhood; which as a child it may have been terrifying for us, yet our spirit is still carrying that condition. We can use the balloons to help us release these events.

We must ask Spirit to help us bring the condition forward. We ask them to reveal anything that we may be holding that is preventing our spiritual growth. Many times people are unaware that these conditions even exist within. Their conscious minds have forgotten but their spirit still holds it. When it is brought to the surface, place it in the balloon and send it off. You will start to feel great relief in your life that you are finally able to deal with it.

If we are attempting to manifest change, energy or a material item in our own life, and it is not coming forward, it is best to give death to the situation. When we kill the energy of the situation it allows it to be reborn again. It may reappear in a new form. Death, as with humans, is actually a rebirth into a higher form. We must release the situation and no longer think about it, send it off. This allows the universe to return it back to us, new and revitalized.

We should not turn into a chemical basketcase by reaching for pharmaceuticals, drugs or alcohol; it only buries the problem deeper. We must face and release whatever it is that binds us to start our own healing journey. We must keep our divinity burning brightly to keep from falling into a negative state of being.

If you begin to practice this mini meditation on a daily basis you will start to see that you no longer need the crutch you are holding to get through life. It has successfully been done before by others and they manage to end their chemical dependencies by following these methods.

The human body is created with a consistent flow of energy and a natural chemical balance. When one adds pharmaceuticals, drugs and/or alcohol to the mixture it throws the natural energy flow off. This is why it is so important to stay on a path of self empowerment, taking control of our own health and our own destiny in life, not allowing ourselves to become a slave to chemical addictions. Chemicals will not cure our conditions. They will only complicate our healing. We must stay balanced.

This does not mean that one must completely abstain from drinking alcohol. Even Spirit says to have a drink once in awhile. It's been proven that in moderation, alcohol is actually beneficial to the body.

Once we become more attuned to a spiritual presence, we will realize where to place our trust. We will begin to understand the answers we seek do not come from a prescription pad or textbook knowledge. There are many so called professionals who think that healing is based on sedating people—that is not the answer.

Our guides and teachers know what is troubling us in life. We need to ask them to guide us through to a clearer path. We need to ask them for healing and clarity. We need to ask them to reveal our repressed burdens and energies—for many of us cannot see it for ourselves? Our guides are not permitted to assist with our path unless we request their help.

The first major step to recovery is facing our obstacles and bringing them to the forefront so we can be released from them. If we leave the past unwritten, it will allow us to create a clear blueprint for our future.

Our guides are not just going to snap their fingers and "poof" we're healed, we have to do our own work. How much effort we are willing to give to our own recovery determines our healing. If we want to spend the rest of our life playing victim, we can be assured that request will be granted and we will forfeit good health and happiness.

If we want to live in peace and happiness we need to retrain who we are and how we think. We must become the Light. This is not something that's done once and then we get to put our feet up and wait for it. This is a new way of being;

we must perform our own due diligence and accept our own personal responsibilities in life. Only those who help themselves will be helped.

Extreme caution must be used. Do not just simply stop taking any medications you may be on without first consulting a qualified medical professional as to what side effects are associated with ending certain medications. Look for alternative ways to wean yourself off and research the best method to be free of these medications without causing physical harm to yourself or others.

Many medications have adverse side effects when suddenly stopped, some even create suicidal or psychotic tendencies and some minds are permanently damaged from years of being medicated, making it virtually impossible to withdraw. This is just further proof of the harm it does to you. There are many resources available that will provide you with this information. Start researching to find what will work best for your situation. Do not proceed with this unless you have first learned how to stay balanced and know how to attune your spiritual self. Be sure you know the consequences of the chemical you are withdrawing from.

It is a much more difficult path if you are already on prescription drugs, some may spend their entire journey medicated. These tools presented to you work best when implemented before you start down that road. However, do not allow that to be a deterrent as many have successfully ended their dependencies.

You will discover how to have faith in Spirit if you start using the tools that are available to you. Best of all it's free. Meditation is one of the best ways to keep you balanced in life.

Meditation does not require you to go to a mountain top or seek out a guru. Nor does it require you to become some hippy lovechild or religious fanatic. Meditation is a method of self healing & learning. It can be performed anywhere. As long as you have a peaceful environment and can focus.

The energy is so erratic between the earth plane and the universe. If you can try to imagine all the negativity that flies all over the world every second of every day. This energy is traversing the universe and is constantly being replaced by new negative energy. It comes from the billions of people on the planet.

As you begin to become more spiritually aware you will become more sensitive to feeling these energies, so one must learn to protect their being and balance their energy.

PULLING THE LIGHT

This is how you pull the light:

> (There are a couple of different methods to do this, you may develop your own, use whatever you are comfortable with)

First start out by grounding yourself. *Sit comfortably with your feet flat on the floor. Place your hands on your lap with your palms facing up. Close your eyes. Envision that you are a tree and there are roots growing out from the bottom of your feet going deep into mother earth. Now envision the branches going out from the top of your shoulders and the top of your head, going high up into the universe above you. Now pull the white light from above through the branches and from below through the roots and swirl it like a tempest around your body. Envision this light completely surrounding you from head to toe. Send these words out from your mind to the spirit realm, you do not need to speak out loud; Divine Spirit, Heavenly God, please surround me in a pure golden white light of protection. Please allow only the highest, the purest and the best to lend an eye upon me or allow nothing at all. Please send me the calming and healing energies to keep my nerves calm and my thoughts clear. Please grant me the patience, wisdom, knowledge and understanding that I need to deal with those around me and my tasks at hand. (You may add in anything else you wish to pray for, you may also ask for somebody else that you wish to help). End with a thank you.*

Keep your eyes closed and wait. You will feel a healing vibration coming down upon you while feeling a calmness that you have never felt before. Some may see a white shaft of light coming toward them. Feel the energy and let it absorb into your being. This is a healing energy directly from Spirit.

When you feel you are finished and would like to return back, thank your guides, teachers and loved ones for coming. Open your eyes when you are ready.

You can hold this for as long as you like, it can be minutes or hours. It's up to you. Do this as often as you like. Spirit will always be there for you.

You will find your new peace, your new healing vibration that will begin to lead you to your own path of empowerment.

You can modify the prayer that is said to your liking, it doesn't need to follow exactly as shown above. *It is very important to remember that you should never enter into a meditation without asking for "only the highest, the purest and the best or nothing at all and the white light of protection". This is extremely important; you are asking to allow only the highest and purest of entities from Spirit to come to you and you are asking for protection. You do not want anything less. This protects you from the lower vibrations.*

You are putting your light out into the universe when you meditate, your light is visible for all entities to see, so make sure you are protected beforehand.

Another method that some use to ground themselves is visualizing they are on a beach and burying their feet in the sand and sending a silver cord out of the top of their head above into the universe and then pulling the light in this manner. There's many different ways, just create what works best for you. Switch it every time if you like, it doesn't matter, just find a method that works for you.

Some of you will start to see pictures while in meditation (clairvoyance), others may hear voices (clairaudience), some may have feelings (clairsentience). You may see loved ones that passed before you. Your guides and teachers may appear. Have no fear if this happens to you, they will not harm you, they are there to visit you or they may be curious and attracted to your light.

Some may appear headless to you, don't be scared, it is showing you that their mind is of spirit, they are higher entities. If you see something that makes you uncomfortable, just send out the thought to them "*you are only permitted to visit me if you walk in the light of Christ*", you are protected, have faith, know you are safe.

Quite often, as you begin to ground yourself, you will feel a shiver running down your spine. This is Spirit, they are prepared and waiting for you, they're letting you know they are with you. The highest of entities, if you are able to attract them, can bring a very cold energy with them. The room temperature can suddenly drop, have no fear, it's a good sign, you've attracted a high entity. Remember, you have asked the Creator for protection, it is always granted.

The exact opposite may occur also, you may start heating up and your body sweating, this is also a sign that you have attracted a powerful vibration. Healing energy is often a warm vibration. Real Hands-on Spiritual Healers will quite often be sweating after working with Spirit from the high energy. This is all good. Just remember to always ask for the protection first.

Do not be concerned if you don't see or hear anything, not everyone does. Meditation is about learning, pulling the white light and healing vibrations. This is the time for your guides and teachers to bring you lessons in life or to show you answers to questions you may have asked.

Be aware of thoughts planted in your mind, it may not be a voice; it could be an answer suddenly appearing to something you have been seeking. This is your time to work with your guides and teachers. This is "you" time; it's all about you, enjoy it.

Start a new daily affirmation: *"meditation, not medication"* and you will soon find yourself on a path of recovery. You may begin a whole new way of life with a brighter, more positive outlook.

You may find it helpful to play gentle music in the background, such as nature sounds, piano, etc. Nothing with lyrics, they will distract you. Guided meditation cd's may be fine but you will probably find them a distraction, the person guiding you takes you on their vibration. They also usually keep speaking on the cd when you would rather have silence, so it may become distracting to you. They can be good to start with, but once you learn on your own you will develop your own method. After awhile you won't even hear what's playing in the background because you will learn to focus on opening up to communicating with your spirit guides and teachers.

It is important to find a quiet place to meditate, because loud noises can jolt you out of the trance-like state you may be in. You may find the interference quite disturbing and irritating. You are raising your vibration; you do not want it to suddenly drop. Find a peaceful location that allows you uninterrupted time with your guides.

Try to stick to a schedule. If you decide to meditate at 10:00pm every evening, do everything you can to make sure you are on time. Your guides and teachers will be waiting for you and they are very punctual. You are taking their time, so be considerate of them. Don't be concerned if you miss a day here and there, they will always return when you're ready. They know we are busy and sometimes we just may not feel like meditating. But do make a concerted effort to stick to a proper schedule if you are serious about self betterment.

You will be amazed at the transformation your life will begin to take. It may happen very rapidly. You will begin to become at peace within yourself. You will have more patience with others and you will start to develop a clearer understanding of situations around you. Your brain fog will begin to clear and your overall health and well being will begin to improve. Your divinity will reignite and your light will start to burn more brightly. Others will feel this new positive energy around you and wonder how you did it; they will want it for themselves.

This isn't something that you just do for a week and discard. This is a way of life. It is a new way of living. Follow this path and you will empower yourself and raise your spiritual attunement to a higher vibration.

This is very beneficial for when it is your time to return back to the spirit realm. So many entities return and comment *"I wish I had the knowledge when I walked the earth plane"*. Well here it is, this is what they're talking about. You have just been given it, now it's up to you to run with it!

Soon you will learn that you can pull this white light wherever you stand. You could be at work, in the middle of a crowded mall or on a subway train. All of a sudden you may start to feel agitated or nervous, you know you don't like the energy around you and you need to balance your energy. You simply send the thought back to Spirit and pull down the light.

It's not necessary to close your eyes, just send the thought out to your Spirit guides:

> *Quickly ground yourself, send down the roots, send up the branches and repeat the following; Divine Spirit, Heavenly God, please surround me in a pure, golden white light of protection, please allow only the highest, purest and best to lend an eye upon me or allow nothing at*

all. Please send me healing energy to calm my nerves and clear my mind; please grant me the strength and patience to deal with the people and issues at hand. Thank you!

Now wait a second or two and the energy will be delivered to you as you begin to feel calmness settle within you. Now, that's a lot better than popping some pills and it works better. It can be done anywhere, at any time, as many times as you need it. People around you will not even be aware of what you are doing, so you don't have to worry about looking like some nutjob.

When you are being told to *"send the thought out"* it means to transmit the thought to spirit through your mind's eye. This Spirit communication center uses your third eye chakra, which is in between your eyes, just above your brow line—this connects into your pineal gland within the brain. This is what is known as the third eye. Send the thoughts from there to Spirit. You can practice this in meditation. No words are spoken from your mouth, it is a thought transmission and visualization, and nobody can hear it but you and Spirit.

We all have this gland. You should know that, fluoride accumulates in this gland in the body and impedes your ability to communicate with Spirit. So you may want to remove fluoride from your system. It is poisonous to the body and totally unnecessary. Do your own research and you will quickly discover the damaging side-effects.

Something else that works quite well is sending energy to others. You can ask Spirit to deliver healing energy and white light to another person. It will be received by them. Even if the person rejects the energy, it is still received by them. When healing energy is sent to another it is always absorbed by their body. The more they are open to it, the easier it is absorbed. Those that reject it are just a little more difficult to work with, so just keep sending it. Eventually you will see a positive change in that person. This isn't voodoo, its natural energy and it is permitted because it is meant to heal another.

This is why so many people believe in prayer. They are asking that healing energy be sent to the person in their prayers. Even though most are totally unaware of what is really taking place in the background. Prayer is a sign of faith and often used in desperate circumstances.

If you are heading into a meeting you're nervous about, send pink & white light before you arrive. Visualize the room and every person in that space surrounded in this pinkish, white light energy. You're sending a loving, healing vibration before you arrive. When you get there, the Law of Attraction is at work and everyone in that room will have a more positive reaction towards you. Their subconscious (spirit) knows it was you that sent it, however their physical mind is unaware of it. This will work, try it yourself and you will discover. Always ask spirit for strength before you get there.

If there is a person in particular that is troubling to you, surround them in this pinkish-white light. No matter your personal feelings about this person, you need to overcome it and visualize them inside of this light. You can watch them start changing their attitude towards you.

> *Only send good energy to another. Remember our earlier lessons; send out bad energy and you will be blasted right back with it.*

These are tools provided by Spirit for us to use. It is prudent to learn how to use these tools correctly because they are what will help us map out the clear lines of our earthly blueprints.

The true purpose of meditation is to raise our consciousness. It is a doorway back to our own spiritual self. Spirit will help those that help themselves, those who seek to rise in a spiritual way of life.

There's no need to act in a holier than thou attitude to be in touch with Spirit, there is no relation between the two. You never have to set foot in a church or read a Bible. You just have to live in accordance with natural law, believe and apply the lessons learned.

Chapter 9 • MONEY, MONEY, MONEY

All money, no matter which world currency it may be, is controlled by Universal Laws. It is a material tool that has been placed upon the earth plane for all to share equally. It is not meant for a select few greedy individuals to hoard it over others.

One should never act in a greedy manner because those who do not contribute to society and those who do not share the wealth become subject to Universal Laws. It doesn't matter how invincible one thinks they may be, they are powerless to these Laws. So you made millions last year? Did you help to feed the hungry or offer support to those less fortunate than you?

This is the Universal Law of Abundance and the Law of Compensation. What you put out comes back. What you don't put out can be taken. Many powerful organizations and individuals have fallen to their knees because of their greed and there are many more destined to fall. They should be fully aware that their fall came from above.

People of greed must learn how not to become a degenerate of spirituality while perfecting their materiality--do not turn your soul green.

People are permitted to have millions of dollars during their journey on the earth plane, this is perfectly acceptable. Spirit will permit you to amass a great fortune, but you must act responsibly with that money, respect and share it.

There are many philanthropists on this earth plane, they have amassed huge fortunes, but they also give back millions, even billions of dollars through their charitable foundations. As such, the money keeps returning to them. They are in compliance with Universal Law. They are deserving of their wealth. It is a journey they have been charted for.

We can observe certain religions around the world that have billions of dollars in their coffers, yet they donate very little or no portions of their wealth to the needy. They prefer to spend millions on their places of worship, valuable trinkets and large salaries. This money is intended to help the less fortunate. Definitely something is wrong with this picture. One must wonder where all the tithes and offerings are going. It's being hoarded. They have pulled the Creator's money out of circulation. It's a poor example of leadership to be following when they cannot even stay in compliance with laws created by the God they preach about. It's positive proof of how they minister their "own" word. One can easily see who the real spiritual individuals are in this world.

Money is energy, man must be taught how to control this energy correctly. One must learn how to separate the greed to be able to allow this energy to flow freely around their being.

A giving person will always be on the receiving end.

It is not expected that you hand your entire fortune over, it is expected that you share a portion of it though. Why wouldn't you? The Law of Abundance states; *what you put out comes back to you tenfold*. You can practice this law knowing this but if you do it out of greed don't expect your tenfold back. It must come from the heart and from a sincere desire to help others in need.

If you want success in your business learn how to keep the abundance flowing.

Organizations that focus on doing good in the world, while conducting their business model, will have much greater success and longevity. Natural law at its simplest.

We should also never be jealous about money. Jealousy is a negative vibration. When we place jealousy on money we put up blocks against receiving the money ourselves. Say, for example, a friend wins the lottery and buys a new vehicle or a new house, or one comes into an inheritance or whatever the case may be; they should be congratulated. When we congratulate them we share in the vibration of this positive money energy that has been granted to them. Do you see the message here? *When we act in a jealous manner, we put a block on the positive energy and turn it to a negative, so the money repels us.* This is very simple logic.

Instead of saying "money doesn't grow on trees" or "I will always be broke", which are negative conditions, change it to a positive and say "I too deserve that". We have to believe it when we say it. This creates an attraction for us.

All money contains negative energy because it passes through so many hands. It is not difficult to comprehend that we may have handled money which at one time or another was in the hands of a person who obtained it in a greedy or corrupt manner, that money sat in their pocket and absorbed their energy.

There are many government and business corporations around the world that are just as crooked as any street thug. So it only makes sense to bless the money you have and place a positive vibration upon it.

Ask Spirit to bless it for you; that it may find its way to those who are needy and need help to ease their suffering. You're sending a positive vibration into the money allowing it to eventually be returned to you.

Greed is one of the nastiest, negative emotions in this world. Many people die because of greed on a daily basis. All wars are based on greed and ego, manmade conditions, which are not of Spirit. What a wonderful world if we could remove it!

If one wishes to act in a corrupt manner towards others they are free to do so, but here is how Universal Law will work...for example, let's imagine you were put in a position of trust to operate a charity. You collected millions of dollars into this charity with the intent to help others. Instead, you decide to give yourself a nice salary with bonus, expense out an overpriced automobile, buy yourself a nicely furnished home and let's not forget the exotic trips, paying exorbitant salaries to your cronies, buying expensive clothes and having amazing, delicious meals all at the expense of said charity. People donated that money with the intent that it would help those less fortunate and you are greedily taking this money for your own selfish reasons.

You may get away with this for awhile, but in short time something unseen (or shall we say; from the unseen world) is going to cause a chain of events that will expose you. Everything will be brought to the surface exposing your deceptions and you will lose that job and have all those items you greedily obtained taken from you.

The first part of your retribution will be dealing with manmade laws, and then comes the spiritual laws. Your journey does not end there. You still have to pay back the universe for what you have done. Remember our tenfold rule? Whatever it is that you took must now be repaid in tenfold. You will not be permitted to ever proceed ahead in life again until your debt has been repaid to cancel out the universal energy you created. No matter how you try to move ahead in life, there will always be obstacles to knock you back down; these obstacles will keep taking from you.

Universal laws can be stalled by one's actions if debts need to be repaid. A Law of Abundance can be cancelled by a Law of Attraction for a past deed. This can cause one's entire life to stall and not until everything comes into alignment, can the next leap forward be made.

If you were told that being corrupt and stealing from others on this side will insure that you have to live in destitution on the other side until you make amends, would you change your attitude about it?

Energy is energy; you cannot stop it from going out into the universe once you create it. Be very careful before you decide to challenge it.

A well known Universal fact: *"Those who steal will always be poor"*.

Those that give from the heart may also encounter hustlers and thieves who may take advantage of their kindness and steal from them, but the laws will replace what is lost and teach those who took what was not theirs.

Always remember when dealing with man, that nothing in life is free. There are no magic tricks to having money fall in your lap. There will be those who may tell you there are, but watch where their hands are. If you want riches in life, then you have to work for it and practice the Universal Laws designed to attract it.

Only those who have it in their charting are lottery winners or are born into money. There is no such thing as luck in the spiritual world, that's a manmade word.

You can have all the money you want, how much of your time and energy are you willing to commit to it and how creative are you? You can ask for Spirit to bring you money making ideas, and they will. They're not just going to make you instantly rich; you have to work for what you get. Keep the Universal Laws in motion and you will start to magnify your wealth. It's not an easy street and it's not going to be handed to you without commitment on your part.

One must always remember that they are also here for other missions in life. They are not solely here just to become rich. Remember that as you throw your life away seeking something you may never find and destroying your very being in the process. You are charted for multiple lessons while here, do not put blinders on or you will fail your mission. When one fails their mission they are destined to come back and repeat it.

Money is a responsibility and one of the great lessons in life. Some individuals think they are doing their child a favor by constantly bailing them out financially. They may bail them out of jail or pay to get them out of trouble, or always paying their way through life. It is not only about money, it is also about constantly covering for them or creating excuses for their poor behavior. This is not to say you can never be kind or help your child financially at times, but not on a regular basis. You are keeping them from learning their lessons of being a responsible person on the planet.

Here's what will happen:

> One day you will return back to the Spirit side of life. Eventually the day will come and it will be their time to also return back. They will return to

discover the purpose of their mission on the earth plane. They will walk up to you and say; "*I am very disappointed in you, you took my lessons away and now I have to go back and repeat them.*"

This lesson was delivered directly from Spirit.

We are not allowed to remove another person's lessons in life. Many times suffering is part of a person's lessons. The greater the suffering--the deeper the lessons--the higher the growth. This is how one attains wisdom.

So you see, we must not prohibit another's ability to learn. This is not just related to money; it applies to many varied lessons of the journey. One must be allowed to grow on their own. Don't take away anyone else's lessons and don't allow anyone to keep you from learning yours.

Chapter 10 • CROSSING OVER

Normally this is not a subject that many people like to discuss, however it is necessary that we have an understanding of how we transition into Spirit.

Dying is a very frightening experience for so many people. Inevitably, we will all face death at one point in our life. When we change our thoughts about it and have a greater understanding of the process, we can let go of our fears. We must realize that we're not just dead and gone, we have merely transitioned to a higher form of life. We are reborn into the Spirit realm.

We become fully realigned with our subconscious mind when we return home. Our subconscious carries all of our previous earthly incarnations and knowledge. We are not permitted to fully access our subconscious while on the earth plane as our earthly bodies cannot handle the energy or knowledge contained within. Our human forms are much too frail to handle this, so we are only permitted to bring what is necessary for our journey. Spirit says we are attached by a silver cord between our earthly body and our spirit body. When it is time to return, the cord is cut and we start our journey home.

Our fear comes from the unknown. It is a lack of understanding of where we actually go to. We do not cease to exist when we die, only our vessel or physical body falls away as our ethereal or spirit body returns home. Once home, we are reunited with those who have gone on before us. Our family members, friends, and pets, are waiting there for us.

Don't worry if you are concerned about reuniting with someone from your past because of something that may have occurred between the two of you, all is forgiven on the other side, those are earthly conditions. The earthly conditions are not permitted in the Spirit realm. Healing takes place, all is forgiven. You'll learn why it happened in the first place; remember that everything happens for a reason.

When we cease to exist on the earth plane the light leaves our body and our spirit commences its journey back to the world from which it came. We return to the other side of the veil.

Our transition back to the spirit realm can happen in many different ways. Some may walk through a tunnel, some may walk through a garden, and some may simply awaken on the other side.

> *As previously mentioned*--the transition from the earth world back to the spirit world is described by spirit as; *"you fall asleep in one bed and wake up in another"*.

In fact, when it is your time to return, the light will appear, you will see it, go to it, it's where you want to be. If you are heading there and see others who are lost, guide them, they may not have the knowledge of where they are to go.

The Spirit side of life is not all about religion. Spirit entities are not walking around preaching all day long and doing churchy stuff. It's not like that at all. Spirit tells us we have jobs and homes that we go to on the other side. We don't have material possessions there, as they are not required, they are earthly conditions, everything we need is provided.

Entities in Spirit have many different roles. Some are teachers, some are guides, some work with healing, some teach the children. Many are continuing their education for the learning never ends.

There are multiple levels of wisdom or planes of growth in the spirit world, Spirit Guides have Spirit Guides, they confer with a higher source. Spirit guides are also learning and one, whom may be on a lower level of understanding, would seek counsel from a Spirit guide above them. This is often demonstrated through Mediumship, where a Spirit guide working with a medium may not be able to answer a specific question that was asked and would seek counsel from a higher source. This is also a way of testing your medium. If you ask a medium a question and they immediately answer you, be very leery of where that answer came from, as there is always a delay while the true spirits are at work communicating with each other, down through to the medium.

There are many levels or planes of growth in the Spirit realm. The whole purpose of our existence on the earth plane is to learn so we can rise up through those realms.

We will also return to a particular role. If you think you're just going back to kick up your feet and relax all day on a cloud, you may be in for quite a surprise. We're going back to work or higher education. Except this time it won't seem like misery. We will actually enjoy what we do because it serves a higher purpose and the materialistic-survival aspects of why we worked on the earth plane will be removed, as this will no longer be a requirement in the spirit realm.

When we first arrive home, we go through a healing process. This process is to remove the earthly conditions from our ethereal bodies. Those with little knowledge of the spirit realm often bring shards of their earthly conditions with them through the other side, they are still holding on to those conditions. The purpose of this healing process is to remove these conditions.

The length of time required for this healing process depends on how we conducted ourselves on the earth plane. Did we have an understanding of the spiritual aspects of life? Did we conduct ourselves in compliance with Universal Laws and treat others with dignity and respect? If so, then we can pretty much be guaranteed a short stay.

Many individuals have gone through this transition quite rapidly; they have reappeared in Spirit form to those on the earth plane within a very short period of time.

If we suffered a lengthy illness or wasted our life with drugs and alcohol, committed crimes against humanity or were the victim of a crime or suffered abuse, then odds are it will take a little longer. Upon completion of this healing process, we are permitted to integrate back into the Spirit realm to assume our rightful position.

Healing is very rapid in our ethereal form. *On the earth plane miracles are instantaneous but healing takes time.* In spirit both happen rapidly because we no longer have the blockages that prevent these events from taking place. There's no set timeframes, every event or condition is different.

If you committed a crime that you didn't pay the price for while on the earth plane, guess what? Time's up! You're going to pay the price now. You will be healed and learn the error of your ways, as you complete this you are pretty much guaranteed a return trip back to the earth plane to repay your universal debt.

So yes, this does go to say that if you commit a crime while on the earth plane, and you pay your debt while here, it will assist you on the other side. People who commit crimes already know this, some become so burdened with guilt that they confess to free their mental suffering. Not all are like this; many are cowards and choose to run from what they did. They can only run so long, Spirit knows all, they see everything.

Sometimes a person may have wronged you or someone close to you committed a crime against you and you wish that individual suffering for what they did. You may not be allowed to witness it, but you can be absolutely sure they did not get away with it. They will pay a greater price than any manmade jail.

You must never wish suffering upon another, no matter what they have done to you. When you do that you are sending negative energy, even though what this person did is wrong, what you are doing is wrong also. Do not give this individual your power!

It only gives one temporary satisfaction to wish that pain be inflicted upon another. In this situation; this high will crash like any drug and it will darken your spirit and cause illness in your body. Release it, pink balloon it, do whatever you need to let it go and know that a higher power is taking care of this situation. No one gets away anything! Have faith, this person WILL pay the price somewhere down the line. It is not necessary that we have knowledge of what happens to them, just have faith that they will pay their dues to a higher power. Spirit has said that there are rules, order and discipline in the Spirit world just as there are on the earth plane, all must be followed.

SUICIDE

There is something Spirit will not show. They will not show the healing center where people who have committed suicide go. It's not the same place where others go. You can ask them to see it; you will be told "no, that is not permitted".

Here's some spiritual reality about suicide. We signed a sacred contract before we arrived here. Those who commit suicide fail that contract. They are destined to return back to the earth plane to repeat those lessons of which they were charted, not only those lessons, but also the lessons that would be charted for their next incarnation. Their next trip will be twice as difficult.

No matter what may be troubling you, you must resolve it and let it go. It's not worth the price you will have to pay. You can choose to fulfill your lessons from the Spirit side of life, but it will take you much longer than if you chose to learn your lessons on the earth plane (the whole reason we come here).

Assisted suicide/euthanasia? Think again! Those dying of a terminal disease who want to take the easy way out cannot play God. Consider this; everything happens for a reason. It is possible that we charted our demise in this fashion to assist our own growth as well as the growth of others. Our suffering may be an opportunity that would not present itself any other way. If we commit this act we have removed lessons from everyone concerned. If we choose this method of escaping our pain, we will be forced to repeat this lesson at a later time.

It is possible we are not destined to receive a healing miracle until we are in our final minutes. Nobody knows when miracles are to be delivered. People have been placed into hospitals beds stricken with cancer, left to die, only to walk out of that hospital and live another 10 years. These events occur on a regular basis, they leave the medical communities scratching their heads wondering what happened. The greater the suffering, the higher the growth.

To those assisting others with suicide, you'll have a price to pay as well. You not only took a human life, you also removed that person's lessons and everyone else's around them. This act would make you destined for universal retribution. The best help you can provide is to spiritually support and pray for them. You will become a healing force instead of a life taking force.

There are no achievements in suicide; there are only achievements in living. You have free-will to do as you wish and Spirit will permit it. But know that there is a price to pay. Your life is to end when it is your time, not when you say it is your time. No one on the earth plane knows when it is time to return, only in Spirit is this information revealed. Mediums cannot predict this, although some try in their egotistical, morbid way to pick the date of a person's demise, but they are always made to look foolish, as this date will never be provided. We return to the Spirit realm when our contract with the Creator has been completed. No one can predict it and no-one has the right to accelerate it.

Have you ever looked into the eyes of a severely deformed individual? Quite often their soul is smiling at you. You may discover that many times these are very high entities that have come down for their final journey, so they have chosen many difficult lessons all at once. These are lessons that will differentiate them from others. They are often faced with prejudice and great self sacrifice. They have unselfishly given of themselves so that others may learn. They are with us to learn and teach; they are here for a purpose. While they suffer greatly through their entire life, their soul smiles at us; they know why they are here. They are great deliverers of lessons to those around them.

Many great lessons are learned through suffering. We shouldn't view suffering as being a heavy burden placed upon us. If we start paying attention, we can see the suffering dissipate. This can be applied in many aspects of ones' life, not just with physical illness.

Spirit once showed a nine month old baby that had died. When asked of Spirit *"why was such a young child sent back so soon?"* The response came back; *"because it is a lesson for the mother, she must go through her life now with this loss."*

An entity agreed to descend in utero as the child for the experience and then returned when the time was completed. This was all part of a greater plan for all those involved.

In regard to abortion; who are we to judge? Those words were spoken by Spirit. It is no one else's decision except for those directly involved. No other has a right to interfere with this decision. Everything happens for a reason; lessons are brought to those concerned.

Spirit knows beforehand if the fetus will be aborted; they know long before any of us do. An entity will choose to go in utero for the period of time and return. It is not an abomination; Spirit knows that this was going to take place. The spirit of the fetus does not die, only the earthly vessel ceases to exist. The spirit returns home.

We see certain groups targeting the mother and all who come to her aid, casting their judgement against them. It is their lack of knowledge that causes them to act in this manner. Who are they to judge so harshly? These groups have stepped over the line many times, even in instances where the mother's life was in danger from the pregnancy. These groups speak their own word and create much negative energy in the universe. They have even gone as far as committing murder, justifying their actions "by doing whatever it takes" to save the child and all the unborn of the future.

The choice belongs to those directly involved; there is no right or wrong answer. It is not an easy decision for any woman to make, much turmoil takes place and they usually end up doing what their heart tells them to. Everything happens for a reason. They now must live their life with this loss; nobody is entitled to take their lessons away.

If you are a woman in this predicament, know that the choice comes from you. It is your decision what you wish to do. Confer with your guides and ask for strength and guidance to help you through. They will not judge you on your decision, no matter what it may be. You are loved by

Spirit and the Creator; your decision will not change this. Do what your heart tells you is best for your particular situation. Remember, there is no right or wrong answer. Spirit will not give you the answer; it must come from you alone. If need be, discuss the issue with one who you can trust and make your decision only when you are ready to.

It is difficult when someone dies around us. If we have a greater understanding where they have gone, it eases our burden and sadness that we feel.

> You never say *"Good Bye"*; you are only saying *"I'll See You Later"*. You will see them again.

When somebody close to us passes to the other side of life, we must grieve. It is normal to cry. This crying is a chemical release within our bodies. If we hold this in, it will wreak havoc within us and cause illness later in life. Grieving is a necessary part of the human condition.

Though the grieving process is normal and we feel saddened over the passing of another, we are still destined to continue our journey. If we continue to spend the rest of our life holding onto this depression then all we have done is turned it into a sympathy trip for ourselves. You are actually doing harm to your loved one in spirit by doing this. When you do not release the energy connection to them, they are continuously pulled back to tend to you. You are interfering with their growth on the other side. You will see them again, so let it go.

We are acting out of selfishness if we continue beyond what would be considered a normal grieving process. Nobody else will want to be around you because your energy depresses them. If you follow that lower vibrational path, you will fail your mission on this journey. Life is Life - Live It! This is all part of your lessons.

Time does heal all wounds and you must hold this knowledge. Time changes everything. Your sadness will dissipate in time and turn again to joy. Depression only stays with you if you refuse to let it go. This is not how it is meant to be, you must return back to an enlightened state to continue your journey. Remove the blinders and continue on life's path. Walking in circles gets us nowhere.

There are many instances of people noticing a positive improvement in their own personal life when someone close to them passes. The one who has passed has a close energy connection and is able to assist these individuals at a much higher level than they ever could of while walking the earth plane. As such, they begin to notice an improvement in many aspects of their personal life.

We must live in the knowledge of knowing our loved ones went on to a higher place and we will meet again. In the meantime, they will come to visit us on a regular basis or when we are in need of help and call upon them (yes, you can do that).

We never forget about our loved ones that have passed on before us, the secret is just learning to deal with it.

Chapter 11 • GOTTA HAVE FAITH

Life is not only about survival, it is also about happiness.

Our center of Light is very intricate. How we conduct ourselves can make us ruthless at times, attempting to get what we desire in life or it can make us vulnerable and scared. How we control this energy around us plays a major role in whom or what we become.

Life is about personal responsibility. We are each responsible for our own actions and inactions. We cannot blame another for what happens in our life. If we have allowed another to control our life then we gave them our power. We need to reclaim it so we can become ourselves again.

We are all born of innocence, we have returned for another journey packed with a new set of lessons that we chose for our growth. As we proceed along our paths, we encounter many unique experiences that generate profound, prolific changes in our lives. How we learn our lessons and conduct ourselves when these changes occur determines our levels of growth.

Change must occur for without change, there is no growth. We must always be aware of this. So many people fear change; they are stuck in their ways. These people never move forward in life because they must escape from their self designed prisons before they can be freed to accomplish their desires. One's energy is better utilized moving forward in life, instead of wasting it by living in the past. Don't look back, that's not where you're going.

Great lessons can be learned from existing in poverty. No one is truly humble until they've experienced some sort of lesson in humility. If you know what it is like to go hungry, if you know what it is like to be homeless, if you have ever stood at death's door or been completely stripped of all your worldly possessions and titles collected, we may then begin to understand this lesson.

It's an intricate balancing act that we must learn or we can be destined to repeat it again. It is our own actions that have knocked us down in the first place, be aware of that. Look for the messages being presented to you.

There are some who choose to spend their entire lives at the bottom. They don't see the big picture and have accepted that condition in life and believe that is how they are meant to live. They decide to accept their fate and in doing so, they prohibit any possibility of a better life. We can all change no one is exempt. We all have free-will to accomplish that which we desire in life. We can choose to spend our time here walking in circles or we can choose to walk down a path that will actually take us somewhere. What do you choose?

Conduct yourself in a manner befitting of one who is worthy and treats others with respect. Remain in compliance with Universal Laws and you can pretty much guarantee continued upward growth in your life. Doors will open and pathways will start to clear.

Remember that when you have been humbled, your spirit guides and teachers are standing right by you to assist. You must ask for their help, as they are not permitted to assist unless you ask. They will help you; they will guide you towards the path. All you need to do is accept it. The life they show you is yours for the taking.

Faith does not mean that you have to become a religious person. You need not ever set foot in a church or to read a Bible to have faith. Faith is an alignment with the belief that your Creator and your spirit guides and teachers will never leave you. They are with you promoting the highest good on your behalf. They will show you where you need to be. If they brought you to it then they will bring you through it. That is what faith is. This entire book is based on this principle enabling you to empower yourself within and not rely on the teachings of others.

You will begin to understand what all this means once you learn to apply this truth in your life. Go into meditation or prayer and humbly as a child, appear before Spirit, asking them to guide you through. Do not ask out of greed or arrogance; ask out of humbleness and respect. Do not beg, grovel or whine, just send out to the Universe what it is you are requesting in life. Remember to thank them every step of the way, as you previously learned, this sends a signal to them to let them know you are ready for more.

There are many poor people who are truly happy in life. Some of the poorest people you meet are the most generous, happy people. They may not have a lot to give but they are willing to share whatever it is that they do have. Money is irrelevant to them, they don't have it and as such it doesn't control their lives.

Then there are some who are extremely wealthy and extremely miserable. Happiness cannot be purchased, it must come from within and they have not learned that lesson yet.

At times those of wealth will often feel segregated and lonely. They wonder if their mate loves them or loves their money. They would never know the answer to this question unless their new found mate never had knowledge of their wealth from the start. Sadly, sometimes it takes a prenuptial piece of paper to discover the truth.

Mistrust also comes in the form of people in their everyday lives. Sometimes true motivations are difficult to read. Who is real in life? Who is present out of greed?

Being wealthy doesn't make anyone a better person, just as being poor doesn't make anyone less of a person. It's all about equality and balance. At the end of our journey we all return back to the Creator and we discover the grades on our scorecards while attending the Earth School. Our life review will determine how we conducted ourselves with our fellow man, if we acted out of arrogance and greed or if we acted with compassion and humility.

Money does make ones' life path easier, as it allows us to purchase material possessions along the way. It helps to ease the struggle of keeping a roof over our heads and food on our tables. We live in a material world, Spirit is fully aware of this. They know we require material goods to survive.

Some people place so much importance on money that their soul turns green. They put on blinders and miss every single sign along the way of life. Some people are quick to throw away everything important to them for the sake of money. This is not what we are charted for. Here's something else; we're out of balance with Natural Law. If we want to attract money then we need to be sure it's not our sole focus in life.

One can have money and be happy; one can be poor and be happy. It all depends on our levels of growth and how we see things in life. It's how we create the illusion in our mind that determines the energy we create around ourselves. This energy is not only around us, it is the signal that we send out into the universe.

The rich can learn from the poor and the poor can learn from the rich. We all have lessons to offer each other in life. We must look for those who are happy in life and see what it is that motivates them. We can have it as well. We must learn to attract that which makes us happy. We must learn to align our life and our energy to a more positive vibration and not place emphasis on the material goods of life. We need to understand this great balancing act!

Life is all about balance, what we send out is returned to us. What is it you are trying to balance in your life? Find in your heart that which will make you happy in life and work on creating a clear pathway to get you there. This can happen faster than one may think when you have the proper tools on your side. Spirit smiles when we smile, they are happy when we are happy. They are sad when we cry.

Happiness and laughter are magnets for good fortune. There is no such thing as luck in life. Nothing is by chance and nothing is by luck. There is a reason why everything happens. A person may win the lottery because they are destined, not because they are lucky, it is part of their charting.

If you want wealth around yourself then create it. Don't wait for somebody to tell you that you are going to win a lottery or hit the jackpot at a casino. There are no lucky charms, there are no magic tricks. Those things will only happen if it is destined. Use your creative genius; put the energy into the universe, stay in balance and you will begin to see that you can attract this desire.

When you learn how to create balance within yourself, you put the wheels in motion to create positive energy around you. This will bring into action the laws created to set us on a path of fulfillment within our own being of light. When we learn these lessons in life we can become a beacon to others. We can teach others how they can become as we have. We must share this understanding with others to continue this balance.

If we end greed, ego and hatred we will promote peace. We will help to create a more pleasant world to live in. This is possible. It will require a universal balance amongst all those who walk the earth plane. Is there a master plan in the works to make this happen? We shall soon find out. The more man destroys Mother Earth and the universe we live in, the more the world falls out of balance.

We have not figured out that every time a rocket propelled machine penetrates the atmosphere, shortly afterwards a natural disaster occurs on the earth plane. We are not meant to be there. Agreeably, there are alternate universes, but we are meant to be in this one. We will never be shown them, let alone have the ability to see them. That money could be better spent elsewhere like feeding the hungry or healing the sick.

It is not wise to mess with Mother Nature, she has the power to make us regret our actions. Nature was designed to keep man in order, to help man, to teach man, to feed man, to cure man from illness. Nature is always in balance. This lesson has been right in front of us all along. We just don't see it. We do not search for the hidden, we only take enough time to see the surface. Nature never lies. If you want the truth about something in life, just look at how nature handles it. You will learn some extremely important lessons about life from her. She always speaks the truth.
If your nerves are frazzled go for a walk in nature. Feel the energy from the animals, rocks, trees and streams. Spirit says to talk to the trees. They are telling you to commune with nature, seek counsel with the tall pine. When you go

for a walk in nature your guides walk with you. Give your troubles to nature. When you emerge, your energy will be lifted and you will feel like you are on a natural high, as if you have been healed. The animals, plants, trees, rocks and water contain powerful energy. This is Mother Nature healing us. We must protect her so we can continue to receive this benefit in life.

As man seeks to destroy nature with his greed and ego, he will soon begin to learn valuable lessons concerning his ignorance of the greater picture. It is our responsibility to protect the planet, if we fail to do so Mother Nature will do it for us.

Chapter 12 • HEALING

There are numerous documented cases of miracle healings that have taken place as far back as the days of Jesus. Christ was the most famous healer of all time. Even to this day miracles are still being performed on a daily basis.

Many people have witnessed miracles take place right in front of their own eyes but they often reject it. They attribute the turnaround to medical interventions or just a mere fluke of nature. They continue in this belief even when the medical practitioners themselves can offer no explanation(s) to the magical recovery of an individual. They sometimes go as far as to say "it's a miracle" but they do not truly believe the words they speak, they reject it.

No man is in charge of miracles. No man can predict a miracle. Only Spirit can say if and when they will take place. As to who receives a miracle is an unknown. We will never know why one person receives a miracle and another does not. We will never be presented with this information while down here; as we are all on different paths in life. Some are meant to die and return to Spirit. Some encountered conditions and are not meant to return just yet. The reasons are endless and we will never know the true answer to a question as such until it is time for us to return home to the spirit side of life and discover the answers we seek.

Many people have been on death's doorstep, the medical profession giving up hope because it was beyond their knowledge to be able to cure that individual. Then miraculously something happens, a shift occurs and that person walks out of the infirmed condition disease free, leaving their medical practitioners wondering what has happened.

There are two very distinct differences when it comes to miracles and healing. Not all healing can be performed in a miraculous manner and has, instead a set path for that recovery. Miracles are instant, healing takes time. We must grasp this understanding when working with our own personal health and well being.

If you require a healing miracle in your life, the first step is to take control of your own miracle. Refuse to accept conditions placed upon you by others. Refuse to allow whatever the condition is upon you to take control of you.

Drastic measures are required to bring forth your own healing miracle. Your entire life must change, your entire being, your entire way. If you want a miracle then you must start walking the walk and talking the talk. This requires working on mind, body and spirit.

Diet and exercise are extremely important to the human form. Humans are not meant to be sedentary, we are meant to be active. Exercise is a requirement for health, even something as simple as walking around the block every other day.

A healthy diet free of toxins and processed sugars is essential to a proper chemical balance within the body. The majority of processed foods in North American restaurants and grocery stores are not healthy. These foods contain all sorts of chemicals and toxins which are destructive to the body, yet people consume them in mass amounts on a daily basis.

Many people are oblivious to the garbage they eat and the toxic load they are putting into their system. You must pay attention to what is written on labels and what you are putting into your body. Many corporate food manufacturers care more about their profit margins than they do the health of the people. This is your own responsibility to learn and not fall victim.

Cleaning up the diet is critical to health. There are many people worldwide walking around with medically diagnosed "chronic" conditions, the reality in most cases, is they have a toxin load and allergic reaction to what they are consuming. For many of them, if they just clean their diet they will find their condition magically cures itself. The human body has a miraculous self healing ability and depending upon the condition, can repair itself.

If you smoke, serious consideration should be put into quitting. With every drag of your cigarette there are thousands of known carcinogenic chemicals being ingested into your system. Your diet will be the least of your problems.

There are abundant resources available from some very qualified individuals who will point you in the right direction for your diet, as well as inform you of whom the bad guys are poisoning America. We won't go too much in depth on this subject, do your own research and your eyes will be opened.

Spiritual lessons are presented to you in pieces with the hope that you are able to assemble them all into a complete package and create a new way of life for yourself.

Every individual's path in life is different; as such it would be impossible to place a cookie cutter package in front of you. The information can only be presented and you are to decide what may or may not work for you and apply it to your own specific circumstances or conditions in life.

The application of the different pathways presented is meant to teach you how to walk in and become the light. This is key to changing ones own personal vibration of health and well being. This is important to all, not just those with a medical condition.

You must change the vibrational level of your body. You must change your thought patterns and actions to start attracting the higher healing vibrations, to attract the highest of energies.

There is a source or a pool of energy in the Spirit world that contains healing energy. This energy is available to every individual that walks the earth plane. Spirit uses workers that are in the physical world to deliver these healing energies.

Spiritual Healers are real; they are Light workers for Spirit. These are the true hands-on healers that have been selected by Spirit and trained to do this work.

There are many charlatans and egomaniacs who only seek to profit from this form of healing, of which they will never be able to tap into because Spirit will not permit it. Many of these charlatans are on the world stages and they will be removed. They act out of greed and the stages are being set by Spirit for their fall(s), they will be replaced with true Light workers. This is unfortunate because these charlatans create a negative impression for the true workers. The true healers know their position and as part of their growth must learn to rise above the negativity that is often associated with this form of Spiritual work. One's intent must be pure to be able to align with this energy field and become a worker.

Spirit teaches their workers on the earth plane to ignore the negative words or actions of another, also not to place themselves in a position of ridicule by their peers. They are not to boast for work done, as they are not the actual healer, Spirit is the true healer, they are merely a vessel for Spirit to channel the energy through.

Any healer that claims "they" are the miracle worker can pretty much kiss away any gifts they may have been granted. Ego creates a blockage to the divine healing source. Spirit will have no use or desire to work with such an individual. All healers must recognize that the energy is through and not from within.

Be aware of a very important fact; it is Spirit whom selects the healers. An individual cannot say "I want to be a healer" and expect that Spirit will use them. That is not how it works. You can attempt to work with Spirit; they may or may not select you as a worker. The real spiritual healers are selected by Spirit and trained by Spirit.

If a Healer asks for money to perform a healing on you, turn and walk the other way. Healing is a gift from above and it is not permitted to charge money to perform healing work. When one charges money to perform healings they are only catering to the wealthy. The poor need healing also and they are entitled just as much as everybody else is. Christ never charged anybody for a healing; this same philosophy must be followed by all healers who work from the heart and desire to attract the highest and purest of energies.

This is another form of the Law of Attraction at work. A healer who works from the heart and not of greed will be able to attract the higher energies of Spirit to be able to deliver powerful, pure healing energy through their vessel into another.

A true worker receives their gratification in knowing they have performed their job well for Spirit and is truly thankful for that opportunity. There is a sense of personal satisfaction within that money cannot buy; Spirit rewards their workers in other ways. They say; *"when you work for us, your needs shall not be so great"*.

There are many healing modalities and there are many healers making false claims as to what they can do. These people have not learned yet, they are still operating at a lower vibration, for if they had learned they would not be following the path they are on. Many will claim that "their" form of healing is better; truth is they are speaking their own words. A piece of paper does not make you a healer. Being a healer is not something you can buy, it must be granted from above.

A true spiritual healer is free from ego when doing the work of Spirit. One must have "hollow bones". The Light worker must be clean and free of blockages. Just as rust must be removed from a water pipe for the water to flow freely, the healer's bones must be hollow and free from blockages (this is symbolic of course). This includes dietary as well as mental and spiritual alignment within the vessel. The body must be free of toxins and chemicals, from tobacco smoke or otherwise. When the healer has attained this state they have opened the pathway for Spirit to use them to the greatest of their abilities. The levels of energy can be increased and delivered through their body. Spirit can transport them to higher planes or levels of growth on the earth plane, putting them in alignment with more powerful healing energies.

You cannot pour these powerful energies through a healer of a lower vibration as their vessel is not aligned with it and can cause damage to their physical body. Spirit is aware of this; they are the ones who are in control.

As Spirit begins to work with the healer, there is an actual chemicalization process that takes place in the body of the healer to align their vessel with these higher energies.

It must also be noted that in most cases, Spirit will not prescribe a course of treatment for an individual. There are times though when they may provide hints to natural treatments. They will never guide you toward manmade chemical treatments, nor will they totally reveal what the condition is that a person may have.

Spirit has said that; *"There are times when an individual must undergo the knife"*, meaning at times surgery is necessary to correct a condition. They do not condone most western medicine practices, so this is not to be misconstrued.

Spirit has spoken; *"If certain medical doctors would allow their egos and greed to subside and allow the Spirit to work through, that many miracles could be performed"*. This is not to single out a specific profession, there are many medical doctors who are sincere and are silently and unknowingly guided by a higher intelligence. It's easy to spot which ones are which.

There is no easy answer when one seeks out a healer for curing what ails them, the circumstances and conditions concerning the individual's recovery are part of a greater picture. Quite often a person will seek out a healer as their last resort of desperation, with the reality being they should have started that journey a lot sooner in their course of treatment.

More importantly the benefits of healing are received in the balancing of the energy/chemicals within the body of the individual. People feel great comfort after a healing is performed on them. This is part of the process required for that person's healing; it is not necessarily their cure.

Now we will show you how to attract this energy yourself.

A true spiritual healer can provide you with a powerful boost of healing energy, but there are methods that you can personally utilize to bring this energy upon yourself.

We are often told that prayer aids in healing. Remember what we learned earlier about energy and creating energy with thought and how that energy grows and reaches its destination. Healing energy works the exact same way, this is how prayer works.

When you pray for another asking that they receive healing or some sort of divine intervention to cure them of their illness, you are creating a pathway for healing energy to flow. Now Spirit is aware and listens to your prayers, they attach your prayers to the divine healing source in Spirit and deliver the energy for which you have prayed. This energy does reach its destination. No person can refuse healing energy, no matter how negative or skeptical they may be.

An individual can reject healing energy, but when that energy is sent through another to them, that energy is actually delivered. It just takes a little longer to penetrate that individual, as they have placed a wall around themselves. The energy will be delivered, so just keep sending it. Keep asking Spirit to deliver and it shall be done. Eventually you will see that wall start to break down and see that person begin to come around.

There are many conditions that exist requiring healing energy. They are not just conditions of medical infirmity; there are also conditions of the mind, heart and energy within.

When one receives healing energy they often feel a natural high from it.

When a healer places their hands upon another and performs an actual healing, that individual often forgets what dragged them down originally; they are elevated to a higher level of being. The darkness within is replaced with light.

After ones' healing has been completed, they always stand up from their chair with a smile on their face. You can see their eyes are bright once again and they are no longer carrying the dark energy from when they first sat down.

It doesn't matter how strong you think you are. The toughest of men has been humbled by Spirit, as this energy is delivered directly from the divine source; from within the realm that we come from. It is as if we have received a "slice of home" and it connects us and realigns us to our ethereal existence.

It is quite often a humbling experience that leaves one more fulfilled than any other material item on the entire earth can even dare to be compared with.

There is no explanation for the euphoric feeling that one can experience, as there are no words to describe it. It is easy to see why people often become energy junkies and desire to constantly walk in this energy at all times.

Many individuals who start on healing regimes will often be drawn back, as they find it their only true source of alignment within themselves. It is the source that will help them balance their mind and slow down the noise and chatter within. It leaves one with a feeling of contentment and fulfillment that no chemical can ever provide. This is what healing is truly about.

Now imagine that you are able to pull this energy on your own. It is possible. We can ask and it shall be delivered. It is one of the secret weapons that one can use to raise their vibrational energy stores. This energy provides you with an absolute source of divine intervention in your own life. The best part is that it does not cost any money and it can be done within the comfort of your own home.

Are you beginning to see the benefit? Are you beginning to see why it is important to walk in that perfect light? Imagine having this every day of your life. Imagine being able to give yourself a quick fix when you slip in the energy of your daily routines. This is all possible and it has been provided to us.

You were taught earlier how to accomplish this during your grounding technique. We will repeat it again, as this is very important and is worth giving additional attention to:

> There are some different methods to do this, you may develop your own, it is whatever you are comfortable with.

> *Sit comfortably with your feet flat on the floor. Place your hands on your lap with your palms facing up. Close your eyes. Envision that you are a tree and there are roots growing out from the bottom of your feet going deep into Mother Earth. Now envision the branches going out from the top of your shoulders and the top of your head, going high up into the universe above you. Now pull the white light from above through the branches and from below through the roots and swirl it like a tempest around your body. Envision this light completely surrounding you from head to toe. Now send these words out from your mind to the spirit realm, you do not need to speak out loud;*

> *Divine Spirit, Heavenly God, please surround me in a pure golden white light of protection. Please allow only*

the highest, the purest and the best to lend an eye upon me or allow nothing at all. **Please send me the calming and healing energies to keep my nerves calm and my thoughts clear.** *Please grant me the patience, wisdom, knowledge, tolerance and understanding that I need to deal with those around me and my tasks at hand. (Now you may add in anything else you wish to pray for, you may also ask for somebody else that you wish to help).*

Always end with a thank you.

Keep your eyes closed and wait, you will feel a **healing vibration coming down upon you** *and you will feel a calmness that you have never felt before. Some may see a white shaft of light coming at them.* **Feel the energy and let it absorb into you. This is a healing energy directly from spirit.**

When you feel you are finished and would like to return back, thank your guides, teachers and loved ones for coming. Open your eyes whenever you are ready.

This process is accomplished within minutes, but you can hold this for as long as you like, can be minutes can be hours. It's up to you. Do this as often as you like, you can do it a hundred times a day if you wish, Spirit will always be there for you.

As you can see this initial grounding technique that you were taught is also the same method used to pull the healing energy from Spirit. Working with Spirit is not complicated. You can reapply the methods presented by them in different ways.

It is only man that complicates things by saying "you must do it this way or that way". There is no set pattern. If the grounding technique above does not work for you then create your own. Remember the importance of asking for protection, the highest, the purest and the best and that the healing energy is brought to you. Your words do not have to be exactly as above, do what works for you (just make sure to ask for protection). It is your vibration, do what speaks to you. When you are in this mini meditation you can also send healing to another. There is no special wording that you need to know, just send the thought out:

> *"Spirit, please help my friend who is in need, please send them the healing energy so that they may be comforted".*

> *Visualize your friend surrounded in a pinkish/white light of energy.*

We have spoken about changing ones life path. The methods shown here are a positive path to enriching ones life. Just as you brush your teeth or take your vitamins each day it is also important to ground yourself and ask to be surrounded in the white, healing light of protection.

If one makes this part of their daily routine they will begin to discover that their mind will start to transition in the way that it creates thought. You will feel more enlightened and that which may have bothered you before will begin to become irrelevant.

There is an overall stress reduction that will massively begin to improve your overall health and well-being within your body. If you are feeling this vibration right now, you will begin to see the merit behind this. No chemical can achieve this. You are putting your body in alignment with nature. This is how it is meant to be. Nature does not carry negativity, only man does. Man sends that negativity into the energy fields of nature, but nature cures herself. This healing technique is available to every person on the planet to cure themselves in much the same way.

Healing energy is invisible, again this is why so many people discount its true effect and reject it. But one would never truly know the answer unless they started walking the talk. Spirit will prove it to you, you need only to ask for it. They will not deliver this energy to you unless you request it. Remember, they are not permitted to assist on your path down here unless you ask them to.

Who in life would not want this benefit? You can choose to be miserable and depressed all your life, that again is your prerogative, but why? It is a dead end street that leads to illness and mental infirmity and there is no need for it.

Happiness and contentment brings clarity in life. The brain fog will begin to lift and thought processes will become clearer. Your energy will begin to glow. Your skin will begin to glow. It is a hidden fountain of youth. All people who constantly walk in the light receive this benefit; it is difficult to tell their real age. It seems on average that they appear 15 years younger than they actually are. This does not happen overnight; you must first become the Light and walk in it daily to make this occur.

It is not uncommon for a spirit entity to appear before you, whom you may have known in this lifetime and they appear to be much younger than when they left the earth plane.

Healing is extremely important to our well being, not just for physical reasons, but also for mental and spiritual reasons. We must heal within before we can heal without. What this means is that we cannot heal another unless we have learned how to heal ourselves first.

Healing is a journey that never ends. We must forgive ourselves and learn to love ourselves. These are the first major steps. Our self worth is extremely important to our well being. Are you confident in yourself or do you have self esteem issues? These are all conditions that can be healed within. They are self inflicted and need to be removed from your energy. Everyone is worthy, everyone is equal. No one person is better than another. Ones social position or net worth has no bearing on their inner turmoil; it's a level playing field. Healing comes from within.

One who manages to heal their being is truly enriched. You cannot buy healing; you cannot pop it in a pill. It is something you must create within.

One must always walk in that light of understanding to raise their vibration. From this you will discover the path to your healing journey. Yes, healing from within takes time but there is no time like the present to start it. Others will wonder how you did it. They will enjoy being in your new found energy. You will be that beacon to them and teach them also. The time it takes will seem irrelevant to you, as you move forward you will build with the anticipation of benefits received and seek self healing more and more, you will begin to crave it within.

Most importantly, you will enjoy your new found energy. This is fully attainable by each and every individual. The only obstacles one will encounter are placed by their own actions, inactions and deeds.

Time does heal all wounds. Whether one carries conditions from childhood, past relationships or someone close to us has passed on. Initially one will go through suffering, but they must always remember that in time these wounds will heal and the condition which is dragging them down will lift, but only if the person first releases that condition.

Everything does get better with time. The energy subsides and becomes further away from ones memories; it is no longer prevalent in the thought processes. The key here though is not to shove this thought deep within. You must release it (this is where your pink balloons come back into play). You cannot heal within if you are weighing down your spirit with negative conditions or depressions, it must be released. As you become more in tune with your spirit guides and learn the ways of communication you will start to develop the ability to send negative thoughts away as they enter. There is a more rapid method compared to utilizing the balloon technique that can be done quite easily. Just imagine the negative thought that keeps repeating itself in your mind and say to yourself; *"cut the energy, send it off"* and then visualize that thought being removed from your mind, put it inside a little capsule and send it off into the universe. This comes in handy during ones busy schedule and enables you to constantly release bad energy as it occurs. This also can be done anywhere.

The concerns we have are only for the moment; always try to think in a positive manner to allow yourself to keep moving forward. When we overanalyze our situations, we lose clear vision. One must learn to control these processes.

Soon you will discover that the negative thoughts and repetitive thought process will begin to become less frequent. Keep doing this until that negative thought disappears; it can be repeated over and over until you have retrained your mind not to think of it anymore. The more you retrain your thought processes in this way, the quicker you will be able to release unwanted energy, with the end result being greater, more positive clarity in your daily life.

Many people struggle greatly with thoughts that are constantly repeated over and over in their mind. Many times they cannot sleep because of it or their waking hours are ever consumed by it. Some medicate themselves to overcome it, but that is a big mistake for obvious reasons.

This is simply thought energy that you are feeding. As you are feeding this energy it continues to live and continues to grow.

If a farmer does not know what kind of seeds he has planted, it will be very chaotic for him at harvest time. It is important to control your thought processes and know what it is that you are manifesting. Use the techniques shown to you to stop this repetitive behavior and send those thoughts away.

Healing comes in many forms. It can come in the words you are reading, touch, energy directed through a hands-on healer, a shamanic medicine woman or man or a thought creation such as prayer or spoken word. All of these methods are similar. They are a healing vibration that is sent out through the waves and penetrated into its destination.

Energy is a vibration. Healing is a vibration. This knowledge being presented to you is a healing vibration. It will assist you in finding your path and creating your own healing miracle within.

Self healing is not a complex process; it is only man that complicates it. Self healing involves releasing. When you need that extra boost one can ground themselves and pull the energy. Surrounding yourself in the Light is an important step as it keeps you protected from the negative energies reaching you after you have released them. It also keeps you in that higher vibration. It is important that you make it all part of the package of you.

Healing is a life path, it is not something you do one day and discard the next. If you truly have healed yourself then you will be aware of this and expect nothing less. You will want to stay on this journey as you will have discovered the truth for yourself. You will live in your own personal satisfaction of knowing it came from within. Your vibration will rise and you will begin to feel a peace within that you may have never experienced before in this lifetime. You will understand what it means to have your heart smile.

Chapter 13 • A DIFFERENT CORNER

Nature is always in balance and harmony, everything within nature grows. As it grows it also multiplies. Nature can teach us many important lessons about balance and harmony.

In life we must learn to compromise, when necessary, to create a balance.

Some people will achieve a false sense of satisfaction from demeaning others. This will afford them a temporary high, as they attempt to make themselves and their egos feel better, ultimately, like any drug, they crash hard when they come down from that energy. This only creates negative, dead energy and sets the Law of Nature in motion. What is given will be repaid (tenfold). We can never attempt to achieve happiness at someone else's expense.

If you attend to your mental and physical needs diligently, you will be able to manage anxieties, negativity and nervous energy in your life. Life will not continuously repeat itself, landing you in a rut where your tires are spinning all day.

One must understand the balance that our guides and teachers are attempting to create in our life. We are where we are meant to be at any given time. We cannot accelerate this.

You may notice that when you are driving in traffic and you are attempting to get to your destination faster, no matter which corner you turn or shortcut you attempt, there is always something blocking you. Pay attention, you are being slowed down from reaching your destination ahead of time. There could be many reasons why this is occurring. There may be a potential accident ahead that you are being protected from. There may be a particular person you are supposed to meet when you reach your destination and getting there too quickly may cause you to miss them. They could be the next great love of your life, future friend or business associate. Perhaps you are supposed to assist another or maybe it is somebody you are supposed to avoid.

When you are standing in line at the bank or coffee shop, instead of becoming annoyed and agitated, realize that you are also being held up for a reason. Every delay serves a purpose. When life goes beyond your control recognize that it may very well be divinely orchestrated. When you come into this understanding it will help alleviate stress in your life. Stress is wasted, negative energy.

Yelling and screaming at people gets you nowhere except showing observers how big of an idiot you are. Yelling does not help the situation because it triggers toxic chemicals to start coursing through your veins. These chemicals wreak havoc on your immune system and wellness and can lead to serious illness if you act like this on a regular basis. You can't control the events holding you up, so just go with the flow. If there are major obstacles placed in your path and it appears your timing is off, then realize that you are being blocked from doing whatever it is you are attempting that day. Retreat and try again another day.

Mankind is naïve to think that they are totally in control of their own lives. Do not forget that we are contracted with our own guides and teachers. It is their purpose to keep us on our path while we walk the earth plane.

You may have noticed there are times during your journey when your best attempt to move ahead is rejected. No matter what you are trying to achieve, obstacles are placed in front of you. You may be trying to move out of your neighborhood or get a different job. All of your efforts seem futile because you end up in the exact same place as you were. Recognize that you are trying to push something that has not reached it's time yet.

When you place the energy into the universe that you wish to move or you wish to change careers, a roadmap is created for you. Only when it is time for you to move on that road are all the doorways opened and the path cleared. Obstacles disappear and you are free to move on. This is part of the master plan which is a significant piece of your life's architecture.

If you want proof of this, look into your past and analyze why certain events didn't happen in your life when you wanted them to. You may realize, after the fact, that your desire was blocked for a reason. The reason is always revealed to you eventually. Hopefully you learn the lessons associated with it, so it is not repeated.

There are times in life when we fall down and we must do whatever is in our power to get back up again. We can choose to stay in that condition or try repeatedly to get back up, only to eventually give up completely. One must do whatever they can to find that strength and to keep moving toward our goals. Every day is a new day that brings forth new lessons, challenges and opportunities for growth.

Perhaps Spirit is providing you another way around. Know the difference of giving up because of your own disappointment or understanding that you are being shown a better way to reach your goals. You may need to shift your focus.

Once we learn to harness our own power we must become protective of this power. There are people who are energy leeches; they will attempt to suck the energy from you. The reality is they are still operating on a lower vibrational level of knowledge, they have not yet learned.

You encounter these people in your daily experiences. They seem so desperate and needy, yet pretend to be highly enlightened individuals. They have not yet accepted their personal responsibility in life and only seek to feed off others spiritually. They constantly seek reassurance and only ever talk about themselves. We all know people like this. Their world involves the 3 foot radius around them and only them. They use others to get through life.

It is not our responsibility to hold their hand; that is their own lesson.

If you are one of these people then wake up and step outside of your 3 foot circle and start taking a serious look at yourself. You are miserably failing life's lessons and refusing to accept personal responsibility. Life is your own responsibility and no one else's. You create your own conditions in life. Developing a martyr's syndrome will get you nowhere fast, the universe owes you nothing, stand up and start taking responsibility for your actions.

Many times tough love is needed to teach people in life. The lessons may seem harsh watching someone around you suffer, but the ultimate reason is that this person will grow and seek their own light, so they too can teach others. It is a repetitive cycle, as one learns, another steps forward. When the student is ready, the teacher always appears.

Some people do not want to be healed. They actually prefer to remain in their condition, as they have not yet accepted responsibility for their actions in life. This is not only mentally but physically. There are those who have life threatening medical conditions, yet they will apply no effort to change. They choose to remain in that condition even though it is killing them.

This is evident to a healer, as a healer is told by Spirit not to go to the person; the person is to come to you. A healer may plant the seed and let the person know they can assist them, but ultimately it is up to that person and many times they do not come forth to be healed. As one can only plant the seed, it is up to the gardener to grow it.

Some people just give up and reject everything around them, spiritually and materially. One time Spirit showed a man who had died and returned back home. They explained how this man refused to accept the fact that there is an afterlife, so he returned back to the spirit world and just laid down on the ground. They actually went over and picked the man up, his arms were just hanging down and his legs were limp. He felt because he had died in the physical world that was all there was for him. Spirit just put him back down, you could see the guide shake his head and jokingly say *"we are working on him"*.

As you can see, it is not only in the physical world that people reject assistance, at times their rejection is so ingrained within that they bring these conditions back to the Spiritual world with them. Their evolvement is put on hold until they awaken and realize what they are doing.

We transition from this world into the next continuing on our learning journey. We are never meant to stop learning. When an individual claims "they already know everything" they speak out of ego and have placed walls around themselves. They have put a block up to learning and refuse to accept any new information; their ego does not permit it.

This not only relates to spiritual matters, it relates to all matters. You encounter people in the workplace or in your daily life who come across with complete arrogance. Little do they realize that they are not going to climb any higher until they open up the channels to learning once again.

Many people will think to themselves; "there is nothing wrong with me". Yet they are ignorant of the conditions around and within themselves. They are blinded by their own tunnel vision. They need to open their eyes so they can see again. A lot of this stems from fear because they harbor deep insecurities within.

Try standing in front of a mirror and repeating the following: "*I love myself and I deserve goodness in life*". Many people have difficulty doing this. They have not yet healed within and removed the walls that are placing the obstacles to their growth.

A major step to spiritual evolution is learning to love one's self. So much is accomplished once you have learned to do this. Your healing can begin, your growth will accelerate, and your divinity will start to ignite. The light will emanate in your energy.

Unfortunately, the majority of the world is not at this stage. There is always something within their psyche that prevents them from being able to admit to themselves that they are truly worthy enough. Their Spirit is not talking to their physical body because of the blocks. It is ones own responsibility to achieve their spiritual evolution. It is where true happiness comes from. No one can give you this, there is no pill or elixir or lover that can give this to you, it must come from within.

Everyone is capable of achieving these higher levels of understanding and action. It just all depends on how deeply you are willing to redesign the architecture of your being and begin walking in that perfect path of light.

Once you ignite this spark, the light will always be within you, only you can put it out. This can be achieved rapidly in life, it is not something that takes decades to accomplish. It is all about retraining ones thought processes and complying with the balances of nature and the spiritual laws that surround us. The speed at which your evolution takes place is only gauged by your own determination and desire within.

You will know when you are on the right path because the day will come when you will be able to face the mirror and tell yourself that you are loved and you are deserving.

To accomplish all these things does not mean that you have to give up all your fun! You can still have a great time in life and do the things that make you happy, just remember to stay in balance along the way. This is the "package of you".

You can achieve heaven on earth. You have taken your first steps by making it this far.

Chapter 14 • MEDIUMSHIP & PSYCHICS

An often burning question is, "How do I talk directly to my guides or loved ones in spirit"? There are many ways. Prayer and meditation are what Spirit always recommends and if they had it their way they would want to see you doing it every day. During this time they come to you and bring you healing and wisdom for your journey. Much of the knowledge is brought through thought processes; Spirit plants the impressions within your mind during sleep or meditation. They can very easily do this during waking hours also, as long as you are receptive to it and don't block the energy.

Think back to the times in your life when you were having difficulty with a specific issue, you will begin to realize that over a brief period of time the answer magically appeared. We did not mysteriously manifest this by ourselves; the answers were shown to us.

You can use this knowledge to your advantage and specifically ask for answers to assist you. This can save many individuals anxiety or undue stress during troubling times. The more receptive you become to the energy, the quicker you will receive your answers. It helps you move along a lot faster in life.

Some people possess the ability to hear (clairaudience), some possess the ability to feel (clairsentience) and some people possess the ability to see (clairvoyance).

If you are unclear in some matters you could consult with a medium, but be very careful on this. There are many frauds and charlatans out there whose only intention is to take your money or your energy. They have no desire to assist you. Their only purpose is of greed and they will always bring forth false prophecies as the Spirit of Light does not work with them. What fools they are! They should start learning about Universal Law and become aware of the heavy debt load they owe the universe for their actions. There is no room for circus sideshows when dealing with high spirit entities of Light. They have no use for people who conduct themselves in this manner and they are not present with them.

Psychometry is the ability to tune into another individual's vibrational levels to be able to communicate with their spirit guides and spirit friends & family. For a true Light worker, this is to be performed without the sideshow or manmade tools.

Using manmade tools to communicate with Spirit places blocks on the energy delivered. Often times the reader is only able to attract entities of a lower vibration, as that is all that will work with them. They are unable to attract the highest, purest and best, as they are incapable of doing so. The Law of Attraction is at work.

Have you ever had a Tarot reading done and have you ever taken notice that many of the messages are of a negative nature? The reader is using manmade tools, attempting to do the work of Spirit, attracting the lower vibrations.

True Spirit never delivers messages of the negative. This would create an imbalance with universal energies of Light. If there was a specific need of Spirit to warn you of an impending dangerous situation, it would still be considered positive to receive such a message. Only entities of a lower vibration deliver the negative. This is why we always ask for the highest, purest and best to come to us or nothing at all.

There have been many gifted individuals over the years whom spirit has selected to work with as mediums, unfortunately as their gifts flourished, so did their egos. This is unacceptable to Spirit. They will not work with people like that and their gifts are shut off faster than they received them. Some of these individuals will begin to work with dark forces, sometimes unaware of the shift that was made.

There are many famous psychics on the world stages that were made to look foolish because they spoke their own words and not that of Spirit. There is no room for the "Great I Am" when doing spiritual work.

Mediumship is another form of healing. It is healing done with words. The vibration is sent across in the spoken word from the medium. This is an extremely important responsibility to undertake, as the medium's message can often have control in a person's life. The words spoken can drastically affect the vibration and life path of that individual. It is very important to be aware of whom you are seeking counsel with.

Spirit works in symbolism. Much of what is spoken through a medium is symbolic in the spiritual sense. They may see a picture or image and relay that image. Unfortunately many of these readers confuse their own interpretation with that of Spirit's message.

> As Spirit has spoken many times; *"we package your message in a fashion that is confidential to you, it is not meant for the medium as it is none of their business, they are merely a messenger. Messages are delivered in this way so the individual can go on their way thinking about what was presented to them. There is a purpose why this is done. The medium is not to put their interpretation into the message"*.

When a symbolic message appears from Spirit, the medium is to deliver it as Spirit presents it and nothing more. The meaning to the individual will vary greatly from that of the medium, so if the medium attempts to interpret the message, the majority of the time they are wrong, as this is not what was intended.

Should one decide to seek counsel with a medium they do need to be aware of this and only take that which speaks the truth. They are to filter the words spoken to them.

Spirit delivers the messages in an abrupt and to the point manner. If your message is going on and on, then you know it is the medium talking and not Spirit. Often Spirit will finish the reading long before the medium does. The key is to find a medium that delivers only the message and does not add on all the extra garbage and sugar coating.

Before you decide to go to a medium or psychic, enter into prayer and ask your spirit guides to bring you confirmation during your reading. They are listening to you and if that proof does not arrive then discount the medium or psychic and disregard everything they told you. You will know when your confirmation arrives, they will deliver it.

You do not tell Spirit what to bring as your proof, they will just provide it to you in an undeniable way which will prove the authenticity of whom it is you are seeking counsel. The majority of the time, Spirit will provide this proof even without asking, as they need you to believe.

Do not be afraid to question Spirit or question your medium. It is human nature to doubt, we need proof. Do be respectful in your approach though. It is ok to give the medium feedback when they have proven themselves to you, as you increase the energy connection with them, it will allow more to flow through. This is not a requirement though.

A true medium can communicate directly with spirit through psychometry and does not require a novelty act. Not all entities in Spirit understand the Law of Communication. A medium that says they can communicate with any entity in Spirit is misinformed, as not all entities are even aware they can communicate though a medium. This is also the Law of Attraction at work--even if they do possess the knowledge; they may have no attraction to that medium. When a medium goes to work, they do not control who comes and who does not. Armed with this knowledge, one should rightfully be skeptical when a medium makes such claims.

A true medium is assigned a gatekeeper on the Spirit side. This will be a guide who attaches to the medium and controls which entities are permitted to deliver messages through the medium. Quite often the message may be relayed to the gatekeeper and they deliver it to the medium. This is why you may hear a medium refer to "their guide".

You can ask spirit to guide you to a medium that only works with the highest and purest of energy and intent, one that will speak the truth to you. They will deliver you to one. You will know when you have found them.

When a medium charges a lot of money for a reading, it does not mean they are better than other mediums, in fact, you may find the opposite true. Remember what you've already learned about catering to the wealthy and natural law.

You must always remember that the words being spoken to you by that medium can change your vibration or path in life, so do be careful. It is always best to commune directly with Spirit yourself, that way you know the truth is being spoken directly to you. There are those who wish something more, so it is acceptable and Spirit does have many qualified Light workers who are true message bearers.

There are some who end up becoming psychic junkies. They can't make any of their own decisions in life or when they do not hear the words they wanted to hear, they move on to the next medium and so on and so on. This creates massive confusion. Wake up! There's only one Spirit realm. Spirit knows what you are doing and that is trying to seek confirmation for something that you know is not intended for your life path. Save your money, that message will never arrive. In fact, Spirit will start to play games with you to teach you a lesson, so beware.

A second opinion or confirmation may be fine, but what is most concerning are individuals who become obsessed and cannot make their own decisions in life, they constantly seek out anybody who claims to be a message bearer. If you do this, you are giving up your own power and not learning your lessons. Time to wake up again!

There are no set time frames in Spirit, so when you ask; "when?" they will always reply with the same answer; "soon". You will quickly learn that "soon" in earth time and spirit time are vastly different! On average, "soon" can mean anywhere from 3 to 6 months or longer. Some messages can take up to 5 years to come through. This is somewhat of a standing joke with Spirit, they have no clocks.

Seeking counsel with a "good" medium can be very beneficial to ones life path, as Spirit will use that time to bring guidance for you. One must learn to use this information wisely and know that they are still to follow their own heart and soul. Not all want to know their future. In time, as you become more in-tune with Spirit, you will lessen the desire to seek counsel with a medium, as you will have attuned your own ability to communicate with them directly. This is a preferred method, as you can be assured that you are getting your own personal information directly from the source.

Much proof of the spiritual realm is given through mediumship. The guides and teachers will bring you confirmation or it may come from loved ones that have passed on. The onus remains upon each individual to use this method of communication in a responsible manner. This goes for the medium, as well as the person seeking counsel. The information is provided as a guide post and one must remember to act wisely, as you may be open to many misinterpretations.

What you thought may have been "the" event may not have been so and you were looking the other way when the "real" event occurred. Keep an open mind, use what you are told as "informational only" and not as gospel. Doing so puts blinders on and you may miss the real message that Spirit is delivering to you.

So you can see the importance of paying attention and not just taking for granted that all words spoken to you are black and white. The truth being, the words possess many colors, shapes and patterns.

You may have received three different messages and it is intended that these messages are pieced together as one. These messages may not necessarily arrive at the same time. Once you do figure it out, you will have a greater understanding of what was being spoken to you. Just like a puzzle, when you assemble the pieces you can see the full picture. One must remember that the guides are not to interfere with our paths, so they are providing you clues.

Chapter 15 • THE HAUNTED

Entire books can and have been written on this subject. There are endless accounts of everyday people encountering spirit entities and their activities in some form or another.

These events occur all over the world. The older a populated region is, the higher the likelihood of this phenomenon, as many humans/spirits have passed through these regions over the centuries. Wherever humans have lived, earthbound entities exist.

Areas near water will also have higher occurrences, as the water helps the energies build. Oceanside ports, lakeside villages or towns with rivers running through them have higher occurrences than inland areas away from water sources. This is not to say that inland areas do not have hauntings, there is just a higher occurrence in the areas near a water source.

These entities quite often are earthbound spirits that have not ascended through the Light. The reason that they have remained earthbound is because they are unaware of the spiritual world or how to get there. These entities remain trapped in the veil between the earth plane and the spirit world. They are what spirit refers to as lost souls.

There are also negative spirit entities that fear the light and remain earthbound in their own darkened misery. These entities quite often attempt to impinge on others walking the earth plane. They do so by spreading their negativity and attempting to interfere with the growth or happiness of the others. Theirs is a world of hate and depravity. This dark energy is of their own doing, they brought this with them when they crossed over.

We have already learned lessons in this book about how to protect ourselves from these entities; however, there are instances when more drastic methods are required.

Most public places have earthbound spirit entities wandering around. Shopping malls, office buildings, train stations, airports, community centers, all have a rapid flow of energy that is an attraction to them. They are drawn to these places because of all the energies that pass through on a daily basis. These energies come from the everyday people going about their business.

This is why we hear of countless stories of buildings with some sort of spirit phenomenon in them. This presence will offer either fear or intrigue, depending on your level of understanding. The older a building is, the higher the likelihood of a spirit presence. It is also not uncommon for a building to be inhabited by multiple spirit entities.

Entities in spirit form can quite often be attracted to a person on the earth plane and will follow them, sometimes even to their home. The entity may be attracted to their light and feel comfort with this individual. If you purchase an old house and start doing construction or remodeling within the walls, it is not uncommon for strange, inexplicable events to start occurring. Just the act of you moving in can be the trigger for these events.

It is also possible that you may have lived in a haunted house and moved; with the entities following you. Their energy will attach to you or your belongings and move with you. Physical items, such as furniture or clothing can contain energy, this is why you shouldn't really wear strange clothing that you don't know who the previous owner was; you don't know what they were like. These items contain their energy. You can test this theory by putting on a friend's jacket, you will feel a different energy surround you than if it was your own. The more attuned to energy that you are, the more you will feel it.

A spirit presence or haunting, can take many different forms from lights flickering to appliances starting on their own, you may hear footsteps or knocking sounds, objects moving, windows opening, or see the appearance of strange markings within the walls. You may be aware of strange smells or personal objects like car keys will disappear. You may have an eerie feeling that you are constantly being watched but when you turn around, no one is there. You may have experienced the feeling of a cool breeze pass by your face for no reason…the list is endless.

There are instances where more drastic and violent events occur, such as dishware smashing on floors, doors slamming shut and locking, Bibles being torn to pieces, items being strewn across the floor. In more severe cases, there has been physical possession or physical harm done to the people in the house. We have already learned that dark entities can cause physical harm. If somebody tells you that these entities can never harm you, beware because that is not true...those with the greatest knowledge have the greatest defenses.

Those who are weak willed and have let their defenses of light down are susceptible to a dark presence interfering with them. Fear is a negative emotion that feeds negative energy, since these entities are of negative energy, the fear helps them build...they are aware of this. Repeating the lessons once again; this is why it is so important to constantly walk in the white light of protection at all times.

Attics, basements and near all water sources (kitchen/bathroom/laundry/floor drains) are where you will find the greatest concentrations of energy within a building. All the scary areas that make for a great Hollywood horror flick.

Certain areas of a building may feel colder than other areas, or there may be a very heavy, depressing energy in other areas. Some places may feel frightening and you don't want to go there because fear is ever present and it terrifies you to enter that particular place. Sometimes the presence can be marked by a smell that is so foul you do not wish to be near it.

The energy can shift drastically from room to room within a building. Somebody may have died from an illness, been abused, committed suicide or was murdered in that building and they have become trapped there. A tragic event can keep an entity earthbound, this will occur if they do not possess the knowledge to go through the light.

If you are picking up on negative emotions they may not necessarily be from a bad entity. These emotions may be coming from the fear of the individual who met with tragedy at that location. It is their energy that you are picking up on, it is what they felt in their final moments and they are still holding this energy. Your ability to feel this energy is called clairsentience; you are picking up "their" condition.

These souls are troubled and need help. Imagine how frightful it must be for them, they are stuck in a veil between two worlds and are still holding on to their fears, this energy continually manifests for them. Help them cross into the Light if you can. If you are unable to do this yourself, seek help, but don't leave them there. In many instances the entity's turmoil is the haunting that everybody fears, when in reality it is a frightened, lost soul.

You may also encounter energy that is quite pleasant. You may hear children laughing and playing or have a very comforting positive feeling from a male or female entity. These lost souls can be attracted to you, especially if you are a positive, caring person, they want to be in your energy. When questioned, they will quite often say; *"I was attracted to your energy"* or *"I was attracted to your light"*.

Some people don't mind these entities in their presence, but also be aware that they are earthbound spirits and they are trapped here. You can help them by guiding them through the light. If you feel their presence, you can speak out loud and say to them *"Look for the Light, when you see it, go towards it. Once you are there, you will see a cross in the middle of the light. Do not be scared, go through the light, your family and friends are waiting there for you."* They will hear you when you say this and they will go if they trust you.

If you are attuned to spirit communication, you can also send the thought out to the entity and guide them along. This same process can be used for entities that are lost and scared, as mentioned previously.

You may also let them know that if there are others with them, to join hands and they can all go together. This will occur quite often when a natural disaster or tragic event has struck and many earth lives have ended simultaneously. There will be many souls wandering around, confused. They can all transition to the other side together.

You can call on your spirit guides to help you with this, ask them for the words and to come meet this lost individual or group and to help guide them through. What you will have just done is referred to as a "soul rescue". If you possess clairaudience and have the ability to hear the entity(s), they will report back to you that they can see the Light. If you possess clairvoyance, you may be able to see the entire event taking place. It is quite a rewarding feeling to know that you helped another in their souls' progression.

If you were successful in sending them through the Light, you will instantly feel a great sense of relief around you. The energy in the room will become lighter and calmer. If this occurs, know that you were successful and have done a great service to a suffering soul.

With regard to the lesson just shown, not all entities you encounter are lost souls. You must learn to differentiate troubled spirits from your own band of spirit guides, teachers and friends of spirit, they came from the Light. So they'd be quite amused if you tried it on them.

Quite often with hauntings, the home was once occupied by a certain individual who has passed on and they do not like you there because even in their spirit form, they feel that they still own the place. There are also instances where an entity has set up shop there and claimed it as their own turf. They will cause havoc and start haunting the building trying to instill fear into you because they don't want you there. They attempt to scare you off.

There are many reports of events where entities have acted out in a violent fashion. The very first sign of a bad spiritual presence in your house is if your animals are acting strange or skittish. Animals can see and hear spirit entities; they are highly attuned to this. Pay attention to your pets. An animal's eyes vibrate at the proper level to see a spirit entity; their ears are attuned to hearing them. If you think your pet is just constantly staring into blank space, you are mistaken; they are staring at something you cannot see.

Trust the instinct of your pets, they will tell you if the entity is good or bad. If your pet is scared or acting strangely, constantly barking or hissing at what appears to be nothing, you may have a bad entity present. Pets feel the negative energy. You may also witness your pets acting as if they have an imaginary playmate. They will paw at the air or roll over inexplicably, as if somebody is scratching their belly and playing with them. This would give you an indication of a good, positive spirit entity around you. Quite often this could be one of your guides, family or friends who passed on before you. Some people have given their pets away after moving into a new home because their pet's behavior became so erratic. This is unfortunate, because the pet was giving warning signs of a bad presence.

The best way to handle this is to flat out and forcefully tell the spirit presence; *"This is now my house and I will do with it as I please. If you do not like this, then you must leave now."* Most times the activity will stop, but there are cases where it does not, it only aggravates them even more. This is where more drastic measures are required.

Any time you move into a new building, whether it be your home or business, there is energy contained within the walls from all the previous people who have occupied that space. There is also energy from the spirit entities who may have attached to the previous residents. These entities may have stayed within the walls after the person moved on because they felt it was their safe haven.

You are the new person about to occupy the space, so it makes sense that you should clear all previous energy from the building before you inhabit it. Before you move in any of your belongings, a smudging ceremony should take place to clear out all the energy in the building.

Spirit says the proper procedure to clear a building's energy is to smudge it. To smudge a building, you must burn sage. Native Americans have been doing this ceremony for many years and are fully aware of why it is done.

Sage is often burned in an Abalone shell, with sand or salt lining the bottom of the shell. This is not a requirement if you do not have a shell available (they can be purchased at some native stores or online retailers), you can use a fireproof plate or bowl that is made to withstand high temperatures. Line the dish you use with salt or sand so it does not crack or burn you when holding it, use an oven mitt or something similar if you wish. Use caution when doing this, as the sage burns very hot and can start a fire or burn you, so be fully aware of this, use common sense and precautionary measures before attempting to smudge.

The smoke created from the burning of sage may cause allergic reactions or affect certain individuals with sensitivities, medical conditions like asthma or any other type of breathing disorder. Caution (in some cases avoidance) should be used by these individuals. Do not burn sage around infants and young children or pets, as breathing in the smoke may have a detrimental effect on their health.

Sweetgrass is added to the smudge to attract positive energy. It's not a total requirement, but it is beneficial to attracting good energy. Different tribes or cultures around the world also add various natural items to the mixture, such as cedar or tobacco when performing their smudging ceremonies. This is done to offer gifts and create attractions to the great spirits.

First create your smudge pot by lining the bottom of your shell with sand or salt, and then add the sage on top and mix in sweetgrass if you have it. Good quality, dried sage burns for a long time, so you do not need a lot of it. Experiment with burning a little bit of it first to determine how much you will need, and also to test how it actually does burn. Open up the windows of the building before you start smudging, this allows the energy to escape.

Energy moves around a room in a circular fashion. This energy can become trapped in the corners, so it is important that when you smudge that you get into the corners of the room also.

Before starting, use the grounding technique you learned earlier and make sure you do a prayer of protection when grounding. It is important to keep yourself safe. This is the same technique you use to protect yourself before meditation. Ask your spirit guides to come forth and protect you and stay with you during this process—they will. The burning of sage cuts through negative energy and helps to dissipate it. However, there are times in severe cases where this is not enough.

After you have created your smudge pot, you can light it (traditionally in certain cultures wooden matches are used to ignite the sage, not gas lighters). Let the sage flame up for a very short period of time and then carefully wave out the flame with your hand or a feather. Do not blow on it. Blowing on it can shift the vibration, be aware of that. During the process you may have to fan the smudge to keep it burning, do so carefully using your hand or a feather. Spirit has given the following instructions to smudge a building which has a heavy concentration of bad energy or possession.

Carry sea salt with you as you smudge. Enter into a room, moving in a circular fashion, go to the first corner of that room and make sure the smoke from the smudge pot reaches into the corner (do this about half way up the wall), as you do this drop a pinch of sea salt in the corner, then go to the next corner and repeat. When finished with the corners, go to the center of the room and drop a pinch of sea salt there also. As you are doing this repeat the following phrase three times in every room; "*In the name of the Heavenly Father, I command you to leave immediately.*" Be forceful when you speak these words and make sure you repeat it 3 times in each room.

Continue on until the entire house is done from bottom to top. If you have a basement, start there and finish on the top floor. Pay special attention to all water sources (floor drains, toilets, showers, tubs, sinks, fountains), the energy is greater in these areas. Make sure a lot of smoke gets into these spots. Open cupboard doors, cabinets and closets and smudge inside there also. Don't miss anything or you may not be successful in breaking the bad energy.

What you are doing is not only cutting the negative energy with the sage, but you are also invoking the Light with the words you are speaking. Universal Laws of Light come into effect; Light attracts Light. Dark entities fear this light. You are replacing the darkness with light.

You are placing salt because it is another method that is used to ward off bad energy. Some individuals will surround their entire house in a line of salt. Negative energy cannot cross this salt. Hollywood does have this one correct. Some people have removed their door sills or thresholds and placed salt in there and resealed it; they do this as a method to ward off negative energy in their home.

As you are walking through the building smudging, you will begin to feel the energy lift and become lighter. It will almost feel like you are walking on a cloud. If you were successful, the building will now be completely cleared of any energy that existed in it previously.

If you discover that the energy did not leave, then check the surroundings and see if there is an item in particular that has a strong hold on the energy. There may be a piece of furniture or a fixture or other material item that the energy has an attachment to; it may have belonged to the haunting spirit on the earth plane or it belonged to someone in the past they have attached to. Remove this item from the building and repeat the smudging ceremony.

You will feel lightness of energy in the building when you have successfully cleared it. All phenomenon should come to a stop. If there were any feelings of fear, depression or offensive smells, they too should cease to exist. Any strange behavior by your pets should cease and they will return to normal.

If you own antiques or have recently purchased additional antique items for your home, it is also wise to smudge these items before bringing them inside. These items do contain energy from their history. You most likely do not want this energy in your home.

At this point, if you are moving in, it would be safe to bring your personal belongings into the building. It is recommended that after you have arranged all of your items, to do another smudging. This time you can do a much lighter smudging and will not be required to drop salt as you go along. This will clear any energy from people helping move, contractors, etc.

Smudging can be repeated at any time. If a negative person comes over to your house and you want their energy removed after they leave, then lightly smudge your house again, it will remove it. If you feel a heavy presence or sadness in your home, then smudging it will help to lift the energy.

You can also smudge yourself if you are feeling down; you can wave the smoke over top of you. This is a requirement prior to performing a smudging ceremony on a building.

You can also smudge personal items. If there's something that was given to you or you purchased, it doesn't hurt to smudge it and remove all previous energy from that item. This way it becomes yours.

Smudging should also be done outdoors on your property. Sometimes the land surrounding a building can be the source of spirit activity. Performing the same ceremony on the land will be just as effective as doing it indoors. Make sure you go to all 4 corners of the property.

It is advised every time you move to perform a smudging ceremony before and after moving because once you are in your new home, it becomes yours. It is your energy and the attraction of your own band of guides, teachers and friends of spirit.

If you are already living in a building, the same ceremony can be performed. You do not need to empty out your house, just perform it in the same fashion outlined above. Quite often one may not discover spirit phenomenon in their house until after they have lived there for a couple of months and then the strange occurrences will begin.

The above methods are proven and true, they do work. This is why these instructions have been provided. The three most important factors to remember when doing clearings are:

1) Invoke the Light of the Godhead.

2) Burning of sage in a proper ceremony to clear the energy.
3) Placing of sea salt.

Your home can be cleared, you do not have to accept that it is haunted and the only way you can fix it is to leave. This is your property, it belongs to you. Don't accept that some negative entity is going to try and scare you out of there.

If you are scared or unsure about performing this type of ceremony, then by all means; there are individuals out there that will perform this service for you. Just make sure they know what they're doing, many think they know and only end up aggravating the bad entities even more. Many so called ghost hunters have been sent running out of buildings in fear because of their inexperience in dealing with spirit entities.

With the advent of reality television programs, there has been an uprising in these ghost hunters or ghost detectives. A word of warning to the amateur; don't play with fire. Leave alone that which you have no knowledge of. Be very careful of what you wish for in life because that which you hunt, can easily make you the hunted. One must understand universal laws before going in like some spiritual gunslinger thinking they're going to kick some bad spirit butt. If you don't know how to protect yourself and are unaware of the governing laws, find another profession. An entity can easily leave a building and follow you home.

One must be fully aware of what they are working with before doing anything else. Are you dealing with a dark entity or are you dealing with a lost, scared and troubled soul that may seem like a dark entity? Lost souls can come across as entities to be feared and what we are experiencing is the fear of that entity. This is a fine balancing act.

There are people around the globe that are experienced in this type of work. They possess the proper knowledge when dealing with entities because they have been shown by their guides and it is their purpose to help others. This may all sound like hocus pocus to many, but the reality is if you're in a situation where a haunting is taking place, something must be done. Who you going to run to? Where are you going to go? Who are you going to call?

Until you have had this experience, you will never know the fear that can be involved. People have been absolutely petrified to be in their own homes because of these phenomenons. Quite often people are intimidated to tell others because they may believe they are imagining these events taking place and don't want others to think they're crazy. Hauntings are a reality, they are not an illusion.

Chapter 16 • THE ROBOTIC SPIRIT

There is only so much saturation that can take place as certain people become more robotic instead of spiritual, robotic in the sense that their world will be controlled by machines, which we are all now witness to.

The world has completely changed as we know it. In this lifetime, many are witness to technological advances that have progressed from stamping an envelope, to telegraph, to email and text messaging. Information which once took weeks or months now travels at the speed of light.

The world is moving very fast at this time. The people currently on the earth plane are experiencing the most progressive levels of technological advancement that have ever been experienced. Automobiles, airplanes, computers, satellites, microwave ovens, television, video games, phones, internet, etc., have all appeared on the scene in the last century.

The electronic world, through internet, radio and television, has become inundated with media overload and a non-stop assault of advertising.

Almost everybody now has their own little personal communicator; you cannot mix with the public without seeing somebody on their device. Many are becoming too attached to these devices, which in turn allows them to be controlled by these devices and the people who manufacture and feed the media to these devices.

Quite often these devices are causing a disassociation amongst the people; they are starting to communicate via machine instead of in person. They are interfering with personal interaction, as many have witnessed when meeting up with a friend. During conversation one will pull out their communicator and start electronically conversing with somebody who is not even present. This leaves the person sitting across from them feeling somewhat rejected or disregarded. People need to be more sensitive to their actions and not act in such a selfish way.

Electronic communication is both positive and negative. It allows one to stay in touch with individuals that they may not otherwise have contact with. It has also helped to reunite people who have been separated, yet, it also makes people seem very disposable. This is evident in the online dating world. One can go shopping for a mate and if they become bored or seek to have alternatives, they can easily go back online and find another.

Machines are changing the concept of the spiritual connection. Where before an individual may have endured and put greater effort into making a relationship work, they now can just go shopping again.

The internet has allowed for a cascade of opinionated people to come to life. Many are very outspoken and act in a tough or bullying manner with their typed words. They say slanderous and hateful things, even threatening others. They are quite cowardly, considering they are hiding behind a fictitious name and a keyboard.

People need to realize that they are still subject to universal laws. Just because an individual is anonymous and making negative comments about someone they have never met, they are not precluded from these laws. Remember the earlier lessons on energy being sent into the universe, you are the owner of it. This energy will rapidly fire back at you.

Everyone is entitled to their opinion, whether you agree with it or not. Not everybody looks at issues in the same manner, as we each have different understandings and levels of knowledge. People need to be more considerate of others and be aware there is a price to be paid for ridiculing and causing others pain.

If you don't like what you're reading, don't read it. If somebody is spreading hate-fuelled energy, don't feed it. This is what they want you to do because their negativity attracts a desire within themselves to receive negative comments so they can act in an argumentative way. They possess a false sense of superiority. These are the haters, everything they say is hateful and jealous of others; how inferior their thinking is.

Unwittingly these promoters of negativity act like this because they themselves are their own victim. They are unaware that it is their own energy bouncing back at them in tenfold. Compound this with the online hatred they have created and these people become bombarded with bad energy.

If no one paid attention to them or fed their negativity, the energy would never grow. The best way to stop a raving lunatic is to ignore them. They eventually give up when they realize nobody is interested in playing their game or feeding their ego.

Great progress has been made since the late 1800's in electronic technology. Machines create more machines. We are all witness to this new world. It is never going away; it will only become more advanced. The technology that exists today will be dwarfed by technology of the future, as the new inventions are revealed.

Technology has made the world a smaller place. People are more directly connected in this new technological age. We used to feel so distant, thinking of a country on the other side of the globe. Now we can visit places we've never been and learn of cultures we've never been exposed to. We now have live, realtime video feeds, which allow us to see for ourselves from the comfort of our own homes.

As the world shrinks through technology, people now have to adjust to directly communicating with others from different worldwide cultures. Online forums and chatrooms now have a presence from people of all different races, beliefs and backgrounds. We now experience different levels of knowledge and various modes of thinking. This interaction is part of the prophecies where all shall be as one. The electronic frontier is one of the mechanisms being used to bring forth these prophecies.

Information travels around the globe at light speed through fiber optic cables encircling the planet. News occurring in the eastern hemisphere becomes news in the western hemisphere as it happens and vice versa. These technological advances are extremely beneficial to humans.

Some people have brought great misfortune into their lives with keystrokes and clicks of a mouse. They don't take the time to think before they post certain opinions or images on the internet for the world to see. Once it's out there you can never retrieve it, it will exist forever. The information is freely available to be copied, never knowing who all the individuals are holding these copies.

People must be careful with the information they are sharing with the online world. It increases the risks for the information to be misused. There are some very unscrupulous individuals who have learned to manipulate through social engineering. These individuals can trick you into revealing much information about yourself, leading to identity theft or digital robbery. This medium has created an age of much higher personal accountability.

There are many great benefits to this new technology. It allows information to be presented to the world that would never have made it there by regular media channels. News is controlled in many countries by their governments. Only that which is deemed suitable by certain individuals of power is permitted to be told to the rest of the world. The internet has broken down this wall. Information can be freely shared for all to see.

A great awakening has been occurring. There have been too many secret meetings taking place behind closed doors in which many decisions are being made by a select few that affect a great many. People are tired of this. They are fed up with being controlled and lied to. We are now in a time of great spiritual uprising in the world and the internet is being used as the mechanism to deliver this uprising.

Protest groups form worldwide within hours and get their message across so others can see what is happening in their part of the world. This awakens others across the globe to take a stand also and realize that they too can make change.

Many radical groups also attempt to rise up through the online world, to build up their presence and attract followers. Anytime a man affirms to belong to a superior race, humanity becomes endangered. They attempt to convince and brainwash others into believing they are chosen.

Information is now instant and freely available. Much information of the past was easily buried. Now organizations and governments must go through great lengths to keep hidden that which they do not want exposed. To many of them this is like walking on an ice covered tightrope. It does not matter how secure one thinks their data is, when it is in electronic format it is only steps away from being exposed to the world, as many are beginning to learn.

The power of the people is more prevalent than ever. Major corporations have been brought to their knees by online vigilantes that disagreed with their business practices, effectively shutting down their online presence and costing them billions of dollars in revenue. Technology is architecting a whole new way of how businesses will present themselves to the world.

Almost everyone is walking around with a camera in their pocket or purse. Peoples' actions are being recorded and posted online within minutes. This raises the bar of personal accountability to an all time high. It exposes corruption at all levels. It exposes personal secrets. It exposes some pretty embarrassing and sometimes quite funny situations. People are becoming more aware that their every move can be recorded at any time, with or without their knowledge.

The internet has turned some people into worldwide celebrities. It allows for an individual to present their gift, talent or light to the world. This platform allows for many individual stages to be created without great expense or resources. Technology has created a venue which never before existed. It has also provided the world's largest library. Information on virtually any topic is available globally, with many different points of view. People can learn and conduct their own research. When information is made so abundantly available, one must learn to filter out the garbage and look for the truth that speaks to them. Much progression can be made in ones life if they use it to their advantage. As we move forward in life, we create our own successes, fears or upsets. New tools will always be presenting themselves to us. We are now in a new electronic age which will never go away, it will only grow. We must adapt to these tools and remember our spiritual self. It is our actions and thought processes within our own mind that either tortures us or offers inspiration. The key is to focus these processes to the positive and keep it there.

Machines can separate one from reality, but eventually reality will always regain its grip. It is probably more accurate to say that if we don't keep a grip on reality, it will grip us; just make sure you can accept what you always see as reality.

In a technological and politically correct world one must learn not to segregate themselves and withdraw from society. Whether they hide behind a keyboard or spend all their time within private clubs or groups, meaning they have closed themselves in and their focus is preventing them from outside learning.

As this electronic age falls upon us, many will have to reawaken and understand they are a spiritual being which should not allow machines to control their life; until then we will be a witness to the mechanization of their spirits.

Chapter 17 • THE NEW BEGINNING

"Thinking outside the box" is such a cliché term; if you never put yourself inside a box to begin with, you will always be open minded and receptive to so much more that is presented to you. This is a truly free spirit.

Some of us are here on our final earth journey while others will return for another trip and whole new course of learning. We make that decision after we return home.

The life experience brings great wisdom, yet there is so much more to learn. We have only been exposed to a portion of the higher intelligences our ethereal bodies will experience.

The paths walked and lessons learned aid in mapping out the blueprints of our souls' progression, which is important because life is eternal.

Future generations will have a greater comprehension and acceptance of this knowledge. It is not meant to interfere with one's journey, it is meant to enhance it. We must always remember our purpose while being here and not confine our possibilities by becoming solely focused or saturated in one area. This even includes the spiritual aspects of life as well. Always remember to stay in balance.

As long as you never quit, you will always win. You can turn off the tap to your own happiness or you can let it run and continuously overflow. Good thoughts will always lead you to happiness. Keep your dreams alive because without dreams, there is no reality.

Now that you have been presented with a new set of tools, are you ready to take the opportunity? Are you ready to redesign your blueprint?

It is with great desire that the words presented to you, have opened up a new awareness within you and have sparked your own desire for positive change.

You alone, have the power to be happy! Be good to yourself and enjoy the ride...

Made in the USA
Charleston, SC
08 April 2014